# A New Heaven

# A NEW HEAVEN

*Harry Christophers and The Sixteen*

### Choral conversations with
### SARA MOHR-PIETSCH

FABER & FABER

First published in 2019
by Faber & Faber Ltd
Bloomsbury House
74–77 Great Russell Street
London WC1B 3DA

Typeset by Typo•glyphix
Printed and bound in the UK by CPI Group Ltd, Croydon, CRO 4YY

A CIP record for this book
is available from the British Library

ISBN 978–0–571–34852–7

FSC
www.fsc.org
MIX
Paper from
responsible sources
FSC® C020471

2 4 6 8 10 9 7 5 3 1

# Contents

# Prelude

The main hall in Kings Place is one of London's newer concert venues. It is buried deep in the basement of a glass-fronted building, at the foot of a long, slow escalator. I have come to hear Harry Christophers conduct The Sixteen, the choir he founded forty years ago, in a specially conceived programme called *Book of Hours: Salve Regina*. Inside Hall One, there is no natural light; nevertheless, a certain organic glow seems to emanate from the walls. The entire room is clad in a fine veneer of luminous wood, all of it fashioned from a single, 500-year-old oak tree. The tree, nicknamed 'Contessa', was felled in a special ceremony under a full moon. It is a magical story and serves as the perfect metaphor for the musicians onstage. Like the hall's architects, they have taken ancient material and, with refined skill and taste, repurposed it for the present day.

The first half of tonight's concert consists of a sequence of works by masters of Renaissance polyphony. It begins with a *Salve Regina* by Tomás Luis de Victoria, and continues with William Byrd, Orlando di Lasso (Lassus), Giovanni Pierluigi da Palestrina and Josquin des Prez. Their works build an emotional arc which culminates in a pair of settings of the same Latin text, *Libera nos*, by the Tudor composer John Sheppard.

It is this final work that I find most captivating. The text is a modest but all-encompassing plea: *Libera nos, salva nos, justifica nos, O beata Trinitas* ('Free us, save us, defend us, O blessed Trinity'). The prayer lasts a little over three minutes, and in that time Sheppard constructs his monument of sound upon the simplest of foundations, a short fragment of plainsong. There is not much harmonic movement, and this stasis lends the music a sense of quiet resignation, despite the increased insistence of the overlapping voices.

Eighteen singers stand on stage in two bowed rows. In front of them, elegant in a tailored black jacket, with tight silvery curls and distinctive silhouette, Harry conducts with focus. He draws the slowly unfolding lines of Sheppard's music with precision and ease, just the right tension, like an oar cutting through water. There is both artistry and heart in the performance, and I am moved to tears by a piece of music I have heard many times, but never quite so beautifully sung.

As the music comes to an end, Harry keeps his arms suspended in air for as long as the audience holds and releases its collective breath, and then brings them slowly down. Applause breaks the spell, and he stands to one side, holding his right hand out to acknowledge his singers, before bowing together with them. Smiling proudly, he ushers them off stage for the interval, bringing up the rear.

❧

This book is an account of eight conversations I had with Harry between February and July 2018. I have long admired The Sixteen for the exquisite sound they make, and for their elegant and inquisitive approach to programming. I always keep a stack of their CDs to hand when I go into the studio at BBC Radio 3, and have played them countless times on air, because I trust their quality, range and emotional depth.

So when Belinda Matthews, editorial director at Faber & Faber, first suggested the idea of a book of conversations with Harry, I was immediately excited. I was keen to hear about the beginnings of The Sixteen, and how Harry has shaped the group's sound and activity over the last forty years. I wanted to know more about his approach to choral conducting and music-making in general, which seemed to me to be one of honesty and integrity. I knew too that he would have an interesting perspective on the recording industry, the choral scene both in the UK and America, and the question of why we sing at all. I was not disappointed.

Harry is a unique figure in music. There are many conductors out there, of course, and many who specialise in choral music. Several of them come from a similar background of singing as chorister, choral scholar and lay clerk in the Anglican Church. There are others, too, who have founded their own choirs and shaped their sound into something distinctive. But none of them has succeeded quite as well as Harry in nurturing a choir of the calibre of The Sixteen at the same time as training up the next generation, establishing a business model that includes a record label and extensive tours to capacity audiences, mining a rich variety of repertoire, and combining enormous popular appeal with the experts' stamp of approval.

I first met Harry some years ago when I presented one of The Sixteen's concerts in St John's Smith Square on BBC Radio 3. I remember it because I was struck by the sense of community and camaraderie I encountered backstage. Harry welcomed me in and introduced me to the singers in his group, and they all greeted me warmly. There was much laughter, too. It was clear that every one of them enjoyed the experience of singing for Harry and with the ensemble, which is by no means a given on the choral scene. Singers from that world can occasionally be more interested in the pub where they will end their night than in the concert itself. Not The Sixteen. They are, as the conversations in this book make clear, very much a family.

Harry's life in music had an inauspicious start. He was born on Boxing Day 1953 in a pub in Kent, and quite by chance ended up singing as a boy chorister at Canterbury Cathedral from 1963 to 1967. The cathedral experience opened doors for him that might not have been so readily available for a child of his background, and it is part of his mission today to change that. He attended The King's School, Canterbury from 1967 to 1972, and went on to gain a choral scholarship as a tenor at Magdalen College, Oxford, where between 1973 and 1977 he studied first Classics, then Music. During his time there, he encountered a thriving choral scene, based both in the chapels of the University, and on the ardent interest in early music that was flourishing among his fellow students. Harry was part of that movement, singing in The Clerkes of Oxenford, a ground-breaking group run by his Music tutor David Wulstan, and in The Tallis Scholars under Peter Phillips in its early days. After a few years making a living as a singer in London, at Westminster Abbey and the BBC Singers, he formalised the group he had been gathering together as The Sixteen.

That was forty years ago, and today his choir is a household name. They are the Voices of Classic FM, and stars of the BBC Four series *Sacred Music*, presented by Simon Russell Beale. Every year since the millennium, they have undertaken a Choral Pilgrimage, bringing a programme of *a cappella* vocal music to around thirty cathedrals the length and breadth of the country, and releasing a corresponding album on their own record label, CORO. They are prolific recording artists, perform at festivals and venues all over the world, have a huge following, and are actively engaged in nurturing the choral talent of the future through their Genesis Sixteen training programme. They are a long way from their earliest concerts in the hallowed chapel of Magdalen College, Oxford, just a group of students and recent graduates singing Tudor polyphony.

One of the original members of the group, Sally Dunkley, sums up that trajectory simply: 'Harry has done great things with the group. It started as a group of friends, and it has turned into an enormously successful professional outfit, which is very well run, and which gives excellent concerts of all sorts of repertoire all over the world.'

The success of this professional outfit is due in part to Harry's instinct, and his skill at surrounding himself with the right people who believe in him and his enterprise. My impression throughout our meetings is of a reluctant businessman, someone who has built an empire without really meaning to. In fact, he talks a lot about how things just fell into place, rather than coming from a clear and fixed intention. For example, it is instinct and circumstance that seem to have enabled him to imagine a more rock-and-roll life for his group than most in the classical industry. He formed the record company CORO not as an ego trip or to keep tight control of his output, but to make pragmatic use of a superb back catalogue of recordings. Above all, it is clear that what he does is driven by love, for his singers and for the music they perform.

ৰ০

In the week leading up to the concert in Kings Place, Harry invites me to sit in on the group's rehearsals at The Warehouse Waterloo, near London's South Bank. It is a busy but typical week for The Sixteen: rehearsals on Monday and Tuesday for two different programmes, a concert in Prague on Thursday, and the other in Kings Place on Saturday.

The Warehouse is set back from the street in a cobbled courtyard. The converted Victorian brick building drips with wisteria, and is planted round with fig trees and lavender. I arrive to the sound of voices drifting across the square, tendrils of polyphony beckoning me inside.

Studio Two is the size of a small classroom, windows stretching the length of one wall. Harry has his back to the light, seated on a high stool, with music on the stand in front of him. The singers' chairs are laid out in two rows: six sopranos in the front, and behind them the quartets of altos, tenors and basses, fanned out from left to right. There are eighteen of them in total – not the sixteen of their name – and their voices are thick in the air. As I enter, they reach the conclusion of an 'Alleluia'; Harry gently brings the choir off with his right hand, and a light flutter of fingers.

They are rehearsing the first of the week's two programmes, destined for Prague, and turn next to a composer I have not come across before: Christoph Harant. Harry begins by offering his singers context; Harant was a well-known musician in his day, and part of an uprising, as a result of which he was beheaded in a church square. Immediately, eighteen backs straighten, and he has their attention. He takes them through a few changes in the underlay of the text in their scores, and a handful of subtle dynamics he would like them to follow, before they start to sing.

Harry conducts them straight through the piece from beginning to end. His right hand gently beats time; his left rests comfortably on his lap, and occasionally lifts to bring in a new vocal entry, close a section of music, or usher in a new dynamic. Once in a while he will lean back gingerly, with the effect of turning down the volume of his singers. It is clear that they understand this music instinctively; there is a fluency and richness to their honeyed tone, and a strong confidence in what is a first run-through. It is almost perfect, but the singers carry their own pencils, making notes here and there, and Harry goes over certain parts again to finesse things or urge more flexibility at junctions between sections of the music. The atmosphere may be jovial, but it is also professional; even when they are messing around, there is no messing around.

Next, they sing through Jacob Handl's *Domine Deus*. They go over a passage for three sopranos several times, honing it. The trio of pearlescent voices are like birds at play, overlapping one another and being answered by the lower voices. The music is peppered with effects that illumine the text, such as the whole choir joining together on the word 'omnium' – 'all' – or a sudden moment of unison on 'exaudi' – 'listen'. They are clearly listening to one another, despite having eyes on the new score.

Harry directs with a light touch, understanding that the best way for singers to rehearse is to sing, and keep singing, letting the music bed into their voices, finding where each line sits most comfortably, and familiarising themselves with the subtle differences in musical language between each composer and each piece. He dispatches rehearsals with the casual professionalism that pervades the Anglican choral scene, an adeptness at turning up and doing a brilliant job on very little time; yet he is also making world-class music with exceptional singers, and the music does exactly what he wants it to do – it reaches out from the past in glorious technicolour and makes itself known to the modern ear.

꒰꒱

After the rehearsal, I sit down with some of the singers to find out more about what I have just witnessed. In particular, I am interested in how they experience Harry in rehearsal, and as a conductor.

Julie Cooper, who has been with The Sixteen for several years, has only praise for his approach: 'I wouldn't compare him to any other conductor. He has a way of getting the very best of you. You don't feel like you're in a pressurised situation, but he really expects a high standard. I'm a "feeling" singer rather than a "thinking" singer, and even though I know Harry has thought through every bit of a piece, it feels to me as a singer that he conducts it totally emotionally, and from his heart and soul, rather than crafting every phrase.'

Sally Dunkley feels similarly about the thought and care Harry puts into his craft: 'He is an expressive conductor, and he is always very well prepared in advance. He knows what he wants to get and he will mould the people in front of him to achieve it, which I really respect. I think he is especially good at making every person feel valued, which is so important. Everybody sings better if they feel valued, and that really shows. And I think the moulding together of the group comes from the top, from him, which I value too.'

Another member of the group offers a unique insight into Harry as a conductor, because he himself regularly conducts The Sixteen, as well as singing with them. Eamonn Dougan is their Associate Conductor, a post which emerged over several years of his stepping in to direct the occasional project and eventually becoming a more regular fixture on the podium. He finds the group a joy to conduct, 'primarily because I know everyone. That could be problematic, but it isn't, and that stems from Harry, because the group is a happy ship. It's a pleasure to sculpt the sound of the group. But because I've sung in it so long, it's imbued in me, and it's how I make music. How Harry makes music is so instinctive and natural. It's one of his strengths, and it always sounds natural.

'It's partly his unfussy nature, in that he lets us sing. If you speak to any of the singers they'll say that. It brings a natural sound, an instinctive phrasing, to the sound. He goes with that and then sculpts it around what we're doing. But he's not dictatorial in the way some conductors are. He absolutely tells us how he wants it to be done, but there's an understanding that it's a two-way street.

'It's a question of ego. Of course he has one, you have to have an ego in order to be a conductor, but it's never about him. He's never putting himself first. He puts the music first, always. He pulls the music around quite a bit at times, but he does it in a way that feels natural. You have to be prepared to change if something you prepared doesn't work – he always comes well prepared but is always happy to be flexible if something doesn't sound right.'

That naturalness is something that Harry and his singers hold dear, a sense of the music emerging from the grain of the voices singing it, rather from some fixed idea of how it ought to sound. Put another way, he is interested in drawing out the authenticity of the voices in front of him. It is a very different interpretation of the word 'authenticity' to that of the early-music practitioners he has grown up around, musicians in search of historically informed performance practice that might somehow recreate the past. Harry, as emerges in our conversations, approaches that search lightly, with the same flexibility as he conducts. As Sally Dunkley explains, 'When The Sixteen began, in the early days, Harry performed English sixteenth-century polyphony at a high pitch, following the work of David Wulstan, who founded The Clerkes of Oxenford. The Sixteen haven't done that for some time now. For me, it has been an interesting shift. I used to sing the second line, but now, I find myself in this repertoire singing the top line at the lower pitch. It's such a different perspective on the world. On the second line, you can hide, but on the top line you are very exposed. Mentally it's been a big adjustment, but it's been good for me, and it's an inter-esting experience.'

It is testament to Harry's flexibility, and indeed his humil-ity, that he was willing and able to make that change, drop-ping the pitch at which The Sixteen performed Tudor polyphony to follow the academic and practical understand-ing of the day.

❧

That Tudor polyphony is where The Sixteen began, and where its heart still lies. The following day I return to The Warehouse to listen in on rehearsals for the Kings Place programme, which includes the Sheppard *Libera nos* setting which will so strike me in performance. Today, the group is rehearsing in the larger of the two studios, with a high ceiling ribbed with double oak rafters, and considerably more space for the voices to reverberate and resonate, giving an acoustic perhaps closer to the cathe-drals where they are used to performing on their Choral Pilgrimage.

The sopranos and tenors rehearse lines of plainsong in unison, an octave apart. I am drawn in particular to the sound of the sopranos, which seems recognisable as The Sixteen; they float, and yet each voice has a top-spin. Broadly speaking – and this kind of technical explanation will come more clearly from Harry in our conversations – there are two ways to sing high on the voice. One can either float the note in falsetto, without connecting to the main body of the voice; or, one can bring the warmth of the lower voice up the registers, making use of the voice's natural resonance. These voices do the latter; they have a fast, contained vibrato which creates a vibrancy in the upper register, and it lends an exquisite halo to the tenors' chant.

As they sing, Harry steps forwards as though shaping the sound with his arms, or painting in air, broad gestures which lead the music towards a climax, and then draw that climax through into a line of plainsong so that everything is connected. The end of a passage of music hangs suspended, but never abandoned; instead, it settles like a falling leaf. Throughout, Harry mouths the words, communicating face to face with his singers. They may be able to see his hands – in their peripheral vision, but they are really watching his eyes; and if he can communicate with his eyes, so can they.

Communication is at the heart of what The Sixteen do, particularly their live performances as part of their Choral Pilgrimage. What started as a millennium experiment in 2000 has become an annual journey around the country's cathedrals. The group performs the same programme roughly thirty times, and when I ask Julie Cooper whether it runs the risk of becoming dull, she immediately suggests the opposite. 'For me, emotionally, it's like a sort of journey of a performance every time, and that can't possibly happen unless you're thinking about text, what you're singing, and communicating. For me, it's all about communicating with the audience. I think Harry is amazing at that, and it's very emotional for me to be able to sing Victoria and talk about the text and connect with the audience. I think that's why The Sixteen is so successful for an audience, because they see us communicating. Interestingly enough, with the Choral Pilgrimage, things can change, and what you think will be the emotional pull of a concert ends up being somewhere else, because of the way it's programmed. It's rare we do a Choral Pilgrimage programme which we're happy to say goodbye to. There is a genuine feeling of sadness when we let go of a programme.'

Putting together these programmes is something that requires particular skill, and the success of The Sixteen is due in part to Harry's panache when it comes to compiling sequences of music for recordings and concerts alike. Indeed, the title of this book, *A New Heaven*, is taken from one of their beautifully crafted recording projects, which includes the early twentieth-century anthem *And I Saw a New Heaven* by E. L. Bainton, setting a biblical text from the Book of Revelation. I will go on to ask Harry about his approach to programming during our conversations, but today Eamonn Dougan offers his insight. 'Harry is a great programmer, there's no question about that, and he knows just the right amount to programme. They're never too long, they tend to leave the audience wanting more, although they never feel short-changed. You can go to some concerts and feel overfed – in the last fifteen minutes you're ready to go – but audiences at The Sixteen's concerts always feel just right. One of his other great strengths as a musician is his sense of drama, and pacing, and that's woven into his programming. You'll often get a group of three works that go really nicely together, then a palate cleanser, and then a big fifteen-minute antiphon. I've learned that in my own programming from Harry, how to pace a concert.'

❧

And so it is that the following Saturday, I find myself in Kings Place experiencing Harry's elegant programming at first hand. I will ask him later about how he put this particular concert together, and managed to guide me towards the emotional experience of listening to Sheppard's *Libera nos*. But for now, the first half of the evening has come to a close, and the audience is coming to its feet and filing out of the oak-clad hall. I am touched by some of the comments of people near me, which seem to echo something of my own experience; and I am also sad, because I cannot stay for the second half to hear more Sheppard, Byrd, Lassus, and an eight-part *Magnificat* by Felice Anerio. I would not normally admit to leaving a concert early, but in this case it is because I have a ten-week-old baby, and while Harry's programmes never outstay their welcome, they do go on past bedtime. I have no trouble, however, explaining this to Harry, who has kindly organised a ticket for me. He is a family man himself, devoted to his wife Veronica (Lonnie) and his children, and each time we meet, he talks about them and their achievements with pride and curiosity. Throughout the course of our conversations, he is always supportive and understanding of the fact that I have a new baby around whose schedule we must organise our own; and this sense of the support and compromise involved in being part of a family is what comes across most strongly when I speak to his singers.

Julie Cooper is the most effusive on this subject, explaining that Harry 'likes to be surrounded by people he knows, and engenders that sense of friendship in the group'. She is married to one of the baritones, and they are by no means the only couple in The Sixteen. 'Most of us have had families over the last ten years, and he really gets that. Our children come to recording sessions with us, which is lovely. We work together so much, that when people have babies, or their marriages fall apart, or they are ill or suffer loss, we know what they are going through, and The Sixteen is somewhere you can be supported. When you do so many concerts together, you can stand and support each other. And it's totally due to Harry himself. He's a gentleman, he's kind, and we all respect him. I respect the fact that he is interested in people, and I feel valued working for him. I know that he respects what I do and wants me there, and if I'm not there he misses me. That really matters to me. I'm not just any other soprano to him. I can have musically and financially rewarding experiences elsewhere, but it's not the same. The Sixteen works as a family, and I feel so fortunate to have landed in that situation.'

Sheppard aside, perhaps the most moving moment for me in the course of writing this book comes when Julie and I are sitting alone in a room at The Warehouse during rehearsals. She has talked about how kind Harry is, and I have asked her for a specific example. She begins to tell me about an experience she had during the group's work on Sir James MacMillan's *Stabat Mater*. As emerges from my conversations with Harry, this was one of the group's many commissions from MacMillan, and the Scottish composer has tailored several solos to Julie's voice. She begins to tell her story, and her eyes fill with tears.

'It was quite a difficult part of my life,' she explains. 'I lost my nerve, basically. It's hard to talk about. It was a culmination of a lot of things. We had done it in concert and had to record it, and I was really struggling. Any other conductor would have had a total panic and got someone else in instead. During the recording sessions, I froze, and he just said: "Don't worry, we'll do it tomorrow – it's no big deal." That totally took the pressure off me. I went home and gave myself a talking-to. I went in the next day at half past ten in the morning, I saw Harry, and asked if we could do it straight away. Immediately, he called the orchestra in, banned all the other singers from the room, and we recorded it in five minutes flat. That wouldn't have happened with anyone else. It's not that he gives you a pass, it's that he knows you, knows what you can do, and wants to get the best out of you.'

During the course of our conversations, which span five months, several things happen in the life of The Sixteen, many of which we touch on in our discussions, and which give a sense of how rich the group's performing life is. They have the unique opportunity to perform the music of James MacMillan in the Sistine Chapel, a life-changing experience for all involved. They visit the chapel of Eton College, where they sing the music of the Eton Choirbook right next to the manuscript itself. And, in May, they are honoured at the prestigious Royal Philharmonic Society Music Awards ceremony with the award for Best Ensemble. The judges' citation points to the scope of the group's work over the course of the previous year, including the release of no fewer than nine CDs, performing to thousands of people, and continuing 'to nurture tomorrow's generation of outstanding singers through their pioneering training programme', Genesis Sixteen.

When I ask Harry about the award, and what it means to him, he responds as one might expect. He acknowledges that 'it's wonderful to have the recognition', but will not take credit for it himself. 'The award', he tells me, 'is really for the ensemble, for the singers and players of The Sixteen. Even more so, it's for the staff in our office who make it all happen, and for those who run CORO too. The Sixteen is a real team effort. We couldn't give all these concerts without everyone working towards it together.'

Team effort though it may be, this book is all about Harry, because it is in his own words. It is an account of our conversations, but it is also an account of his life in music, which stretches back to his earliest days in Kent, and on into the future. It encompasses his work in America, at the helm of the Handel and Haydn Society in Boston, and his commitment to the next generation of singers. It focuses on his approach to choral conducting, and to the music he is drawn to. And above all, it makes clear the extent to which making music, for him, is an act of friendship. I cannot think of a more laudable reason for placing music at the centre of one's life.

Our intention was for this book to be accessible to anyone with an interest in music, be they amateur, professional, musically literate or a complete newcomer to the subject. As a result, while we have used some technical terms, we have done our best to explain them in plain English, describing music in such a way that anyone might be able to imagine its sound. We began each of our conversations with a choral work; Harry chose them from his recording catalogue as starting-points for our discussions. They range from early Tudor polyphony to the music of the present day, and I have listed the recordings at the end of the book, in case readers are inspired to listen too.

The conversations flowed easily, but occasionally veered off-topic, so I have edited them slightly and moved things around to make more sense on the page. Throughout the project, Harry was good-humoured, open, rigorous and unflappable, and made me feel part of the family. These are the qualities that make him such a successful conductor and compelling musician, and I hope that I have done his words justice.

# ONE
# Musical Beginnings
# (Part One)

The 10.22 from London Victoria to Canterbury passes steadily through south London and, as the city dwindles, continues on through the Kent countryside. It is a miserable day in February, and though the train is heated, I keep my coat on.

Harry has invited me to his home in the Kent village of Otford for the first of our conversations. For my homework, he has pointed me in the direction of one of the best-loved Tudor anthems: *O nata lux*, by Thomas Tallis. As I listen on the train, I am struck by the brilliance of sound he achieves with The Sixteen. It is full and rich, but also balanced and controlled, and Harry seems to delight in every false relation (those juicy and expressive harmonic clashes between the major and minor third of a chord, a feature of Tallis and indeed Tudor church music in general – we will talk more about false relations later).

Harry picks me up from the station and drives me to his home. The house is halfway up a steep private road and it feels ancient, set back from the road in a slight dip, nestled and safe, with the warm familiarity of an English inn. In fact, it is relatively new, built in the 1950s by a man returning from New Zealand who craved verandas and expansive views. As I will discover when we sit down to talk in the conservatory at the back of the house, he designed it to look over a long and peaceful garden, and out to the Downs beyond.

As we approach the front door, Harry tells me he finds his home a haven to return to, even if only for one night, a welcome respite from a musician's life on the road. We will talk in later conversations about his touring life; but for now, we begin with music.

🔖

*Harry, on my journey here, I was listening to your recording of* O nata lux *by Tallis. Interestingly, Tallis had a couple of early jobs in this part of the world; first of all at Dover Priory and then Canterbury Cathedral.*

Yes, he was probably born in Kent, like me, and was briefly at Dover Priory. He then became what they called a 'vicar choral' at Canterbury Cathedral, after it had ceased to be a Benedictine monastery. It's thought he spent two years there before going on to the Chapel Royal.

O nata lux *is a piece I know well – short and simple. But in your recording I was struck for perhaps the first time by the strength of contrast between the extreme purity of 'light from light', and the rich dissonance that comes in when the text talks about the body of Christ. You manage to get both the lucidity and the depth across so clearly with* The Sixteen.

It's a real gem of a choral piece. It contains several false relations, which in Victorian editions they ironed out because they thought them hideous. Now, of course, we know what a beautiful feature they are. The thing with all of that Tudor repertoire is that the better composers – like Byrd and Tallis

– do it all for you, particularly in the sonorities of the middle textures. In that recording I do it at high pitch . . .

*Yes, it sounds high. At one point I wasn't sure if your top line was sopranos or boy trebles . . .*

It is sung by sopranos, but I have to say the sopranos in the group hate me for it, particularly when I start a programme with *O nata lux* at that pitch. The piece is short, but it has to be absolutely perfect, and you're right, it has to have a phenomenal sonority in the opening section. The last six bars repeat, and they're also soft and mesmeric, a simple chant. In performance, I sometimes linger for a long time over the final dissonance at the end. I remember David Wulstan in Oxford [founder and conductor of The Clerkes of Oxenford, one of the first modern groups to perform Tudor polyphony] used to relish those false relations. He used to conduct away, and then stop on the clash, and a grin would come over his face before he started again. False relations are part of Tudor music, and you either touch on them, or you make them a real feature and drive into them.

*That, I suppose, is the unique privilege of the conductor. Do you remember the first time you heard or sang* O nata lux?

It will have been in Canterbury Cathedral as a chorister. It wasn't until many years later I realised that I'd been singing that music in the very same building where Tallis himself sang. And I was very lucky to have ended up there. After all, I was born in a pub . . .

*In Kent?*

Yes, near Goudhurst in the Weald of Kent, an area known as the 'Garden of England', about twenty-five miles south of here. We're on the edge of the North Downs here, and the big dip between the North and South Downs is the Weald. There are lots of gorgeous villages whose names end in –den, like Tenterden, and others whose names end in –hurst, like Staplehurst and Goudhurst. My father ran a little pub that's still there today. In my day it was a Fremlin's pub, a Kent brewery that was later taken over by Whitbread. We were surrounded by hop fields that don't exist today. At the end of August and beginning of September, men and women from the East End of London and students from abroad would all arrive to pick the hops, and there was a real feeling of community. Dad would invite the East Enders in, whereas the local farmers all thought they were crooks. The locals gave him quite a lot of grief for it, but Dad was an East Ender too, born within the sound of Bow Bells, so he invited them in. Until I was eight or nine, that was my life.

*Were there any musicians in the family?*

Not really, but my mother loved music and played the piano. She came from a well-off family, and was one of four daughters. She married my father during the war and they ran the pub together.

*So how did you end up going to sing as a chorister at Canterbury Cathedral?*

The pub got taken over by another brewery, and we had to move to Canterbury. My parents found and bought a little tobacconist and sweet shop on Castle Street, about ten minutes' walk from the cathedral. And then they had to decide where I would go to school. My brothers were at the secondary stage already, but I was younger. My parents asked a teacher at my school in Goudhurst where to send me, and he told them that it was worth putting me forward for the choir school, because I had a nice voice and could read well. He meant books, not music. The choir school at Canterbury had about forty students, both boarders and day boys. I remember Dad driving me up for an audition, which took place in a little library. I had to sing a hymn tune and read a psalm out loud. I wasn't confounded by words like 'confoundeth' – it seemed easy to me. So I got in, and my life changed completely.

*Looking back on your entry into that Anglican cathedral world, an environment that must now be so familiar to you, do you remember if it felt alien at all, and was hard to adjust to?*
No. I loved every minute of it, and found it fascinating. Of course, you don't appreciate where you are as a child; but the cathedral was our playground. We had to be professional and sing the services, but once we got our cassocks and surplices off, all hell would break loose. Some people had grim experiences of choir school and being away from home, but I didn't. I lived ten minutes away. And it also depends on who's in charge. I was so lucky that Allan Wicks was the organist and choirmaster at Canterbury [from 1961 to 1988]. He was a real maverick. He'd been an organ scholar at Christ Church Cathedral in Oxford and organist at Manchester Cathedral before being appointed in Canterbury, but he

didn't conform. He was the first person to play the music of French composer Olivier Messiaen in England, and performed György Ligeti's *Volumina* at the Royal Festival Hall. And he brought modern music to Canterbury, composers like Peter Maxwell Davies and Michael Tippett. I remember we sang a piece by Tippett which was known as the 'yellow peril' – it had a yellow cover and was incredibly difficult. Allan had a different way of doing things to the usual Anglican way. He wasn't so much interested in achieving perfect blend and tuning; what he wanted was for children to sing. That sounds so simple, but it's exactly what I've done with my group all through the years: encouraging them to sing, and not to put up barriers before they have even started.

*But the Anglican choral education, as wonderful as it is, can inadvertently create barriers for young singers, can't it? You're learning to use your voice, to sight-read, and are steeped in a daily tradition, all of which is positive. But you're also standing in a physically restrictive position, sandwiched between two wooden pews, facing your fellow singers but twisting your neck to see the conductor; and you're being required to show up and deliver something perfect straight away, which can often lead to singers holding back. So I'm interested that your early experience wasn't of that kind of restriction, but instead of someone who really encouraged you to sing out.*

Yes, I was very lucky. One great thing that Allan did was to make us sing arias instead of mediocre anthems written by cathedral organists, as would happen up and down the country. All the boys would sing the aria in unison – all thirty-six of us. These were arias from great oratorios and cantatas, like 'I know that my Redeemer liveth' from Handel's *Messiah*, and 'Buß und Reu' from Bach's *St Matthew Passion*. I remember we even once did the whole first movement of Mozart's solo motet, *Exsultate, jubilate*.

*Did he do that in order to introduce you to that repertoire?*
Yes, but also to make us sing music that had a real line. The more mediocre anthems we could have sung may have had a nice tune, but they never had line in the way those great arias did. Allan was always getting us to sing in phrases. I remember once we were rehearsing in the Quire at about eight o'clock on a Friday morning, and we weren't singing well. And he said, 'I want you to sing like *this*' – and he took a book of Psalms and flung it into the air, and it soared across the Quire. We realised he was telling us to shape the phrase, and to fill the building with sound. It was all about the architecture of phrases, which influences everything I do today. He made everything sound great: Bach, which he loved; Tudor music, which he later admitted to me that he didn't really understand; even Anglican chant, which can be rather dull . . .

*. . . except when it's flying through the building like a book of Psalms . . .*
Exactly. Allan made everything feel natural. So, if we were singing badly, or our attention was wandering, he'd click his fingers and make us stand up straight – but it never felt false. In rehearsals he always knew when we needed to let off steam; he'd tell us to take a break, and we'd be clambering over beams, leaping over the stalls in the practice rooms, and

then we'd be back and really paying attention. If there was a hideous mistake during a service, you knew you were in for something special. With most cathedral conductors, if something goes wrong, that's it: it's ruined and you're in trouble. But with Allan, he would turn on the magic a few bars later, so you and the whole congregation would go away thinking it had been something really special. Of course, you might be hauled up afterwards and told off for getting your fourths or fifths wrong.

*You do seem to remember all this incredibly well. It's funny how important those early singing experiences are for anyone who ends up involved in music in any way later in life. It's as though they become your DNA, a profound imprint. Is there certain music you encountered in Canterbury that went on to shape your musical curiosity and your career?*

Well, yes, the Renaissance repertoire. I remember those works being difficult for Allan, but him really making something of them. I'm thinking of anthems by Orlando Gibbons, Tallis and Byrd – the staple diet of English Tudor music. Although he didn't understand the music as we do today, he understood its architecture, and that's something that, as I said before, really influences me today. I feel that those buildings and the shape of the music go hand in hand. I think of Canterbury Cathedral on a dark winter's evening – it was so atmospheric. We had the run of the place, and after Evensong I'd wander round the building, perhaps cycle through the cloisters before going home. I also came out of Canterbury adoring Benjamin Britten. I particularly loved the *Hymn of St Columba*.

*Britten is so interesting because his music – as with so much of the Anglican repertoire – is written and tailored for young voices. It's not music written for adults that children are trying to sing. You have a sort of ownership of the music, and it sits so beautifully on the voice.*

It does. And I think everyone remembers the first time they sang *A Ceremony of Carols*, don't they? I remember mine. It was in Canterbury, and we were doing a BBC broadcast, and it was an amazing experience. We really dug into the notes, and made such a gutsy sound in 'This little babe'. Allan wasn't a wishy-washy conductor with what I call an 'organist's beat'. He also wasn't one of those Anglican conductors who care only about how to end a piece, which can lead to the endings of phrases feeling very fussy. I don't know if Allan ever trained as a conductor, but he was a proper one. He ran Canterbury Choral Society, where he conducted works like Gustav Mahler's Symphony no. 8 [in 1973]. I don't know if this is true, but people who knew Allan say they see bits of his way of conducting when they watch me. Whatever we were doing – responses, a psalm, a hymn – there was a moment of preparation. Other conductors just care if everyone stands up at the same time, all regimented; Allan cared that we breathed together, poised, like the violin bows in an orchestra. He would often say 'bow on the string', to get us to prepare properly. He often talked in orchestral terms to us, and we understood because we were all learning orchestral instruments.

*What was your instrument?*

Clarinet. I loved it – all the way through to university, at which point I had to make a choice between playing the clarinet and singing, and I chose singing. I remember Johnny Dankworth [Sir John Dankworth, jazz composer, saxophonist and clarinettist] once saying that he'd been at the Royal College of Music, and that he'd wanted to be a classical clarinettist, but that he'd turned to jazz because his competition was none other than Colin Davis [Sir Colin Davis, celebrated conductor, who started off as a clarinettist]. Well, I was at school with Andrew Marriner [son of conductor Sir Neville Marriner, and the long-standing principal clarinet of the London Symphony Orchestra] . . .

*So at what point did you graduate up to The King's School, Canterbury?*
I think I was about twelve or thirteen. I didn't want to leave the choir school so early, but my voice was breaking and I had to leave. The choir school was very separate from King's, but a lot of people did go on there, which is part of the reason why the music was so good at King's. As shopkeepers, my parents couldn't afford to send me to King's, but I got a scholarship which covered part of my fees, and the Cathedral paid the rest. I'm pretty sure Allan had something to do with that. It's why I have such a strong relationship with Canterbury Cathedral to this day.

*So when you stopped being a chorister at the cathedral, where did you do your singing?*
In The King's School, which had a choir run by Edred Wright [the school's Director of Music from 1958 to 1979]. In the same way as Allan, he encouraged people. He wasn't a dictator. This was a public school in the late 1960s, early 1970s, and

unusually for that time we called him Edred, and he called us by our first names. He encouraged us to sing in barbershop groups, to play chamber music together, and all this under the reign of a headmaster who had no time for music.

*So what kind of music did Edred have you sing in choir?*
Our school services on a Sunday took place in the cathedral, and during those we sang standard Anglican repertoire. But we also had a glee club that sang real Victoriana, and a madrigal club that sang pieces like the Britten *Flower Songs*, which are very little known today. I suppose it showed the quality of the school choir that we could sing works like that. We regularly had four students gaining choral scholarships to Oxbridge each year. Choral music was Edred's forte, but we also had an accomplished orchestra, from which students graduated to the National Youth Orchestra. I had the chance to play symphonies by Jean Sibelius, which was wonderful.

I struggled academically at King's, but I loved music. I practised a lot at home. There was a room off the back of our shop that led on to the kitchen and an outside loo at the back. We called it 'The Room', and it was where the family did everything. My father was a big man who smoked, and loved the racing. Every day he would sneak off to the betting shop, but tell my mother he was going to the Post Office. Afterwards, he would sit at one end of The Room with his little television, watching the racing and smoking a cigar – he used to inhale them. Then there was a round table in the middle of The Room where we ate, and at the other end another television which my brother Ronnie watched at full volume. Ronnie was five years older than me and had Down's syndrome, and he'd create merry hell if we tried to turn his television down. I also did my homework in The Room, practised my clarinet and sometimes tried to practise my singing too. Can you imagine the noise? My wife Lonnie gets annoyed with me because I'm able to completely divorce myself from noise. If there's a racket going on I can focus in on something else and block it out.

*But the thing that you were focusing on in those days was music. Did you have any sense then that you wanted to go on and pursue music as a career?*

No, not really, I didn't know what I wanted to do. It's so different today. I look at my own children, and there's so much pressure. Back then there was pressure to get through school, but you didn't think about the next year. You did your 'O' levels, then found yourself in the sixth form for 'A' levels . . . Sixth form for me was a nightmare, because I had no idea what I wanted to do. I don't even think I'd studied Music at 'O' level. I remember starting History, Economics and English for 'A' level, and I did about half a term of that. I couldn't understand a thing about economics, and I really wasn't up to speed with history like the other bright sparks in the class, so I changed to Latin, Greek and Ancient History. And then the Master told me I had to keep on one of the subjects I had started, so I kept on with English. I don't know why my mother didn't kick up a fuss and tell me to stick with three rather than four subjects, because I struggled. Funnily enough, The Sixteen were performing Vivaldi's *Gloria* in a concert in Rochester the other day, and afterwards a man came up to me and said: 'You won't remember me, but we were at King's doing Classics 'A' levels together.' And he remembered that I used to get all my books and pile them high on my desk and hide behind them so that our teacher, Mr Mackintosh, couldn't ask me a question. He used to come over to me and move the books and say, 'Come on, Christophers, you're in there somewhere!' Upstairs in the loft I have a school report, the kind they couldn't write today, which says: 'I do believe Christophers has a brain, but I've yet to find the crowbar.'

*So music wasn't something you studied academically – it was your extra-curricular activity, your enjoyment.*
Yes, it was my hobby, really. It got me out of the house, too. I had the school cathedral service on a Sunday, and then orchestra after that, and invariably in the sixth form I'd end up going back into school a lot to see my friends who were boarders, and go to the pub or listen to music in secret.

*After King's School, you went to Magdalen College, Oxford. That's quite a trajectory.*
Yes, I was very lucky. At King's, Edred Wright also gave us singing lessons – nothing too technical, but we did a lot of singing, and our sight-reading was of a high standard. He had quite a good track record of getting boys choral scholarships to Oxbridge, and he suggested I go for one. The auditions happened in September. My academic abilities were not brilliant, but in those days it didn't matter. If you could sing, play cricket, row or were a good actor it didn't really matter about your 'A' levels – not like today.

In those days the Cambridge and Oxford choral trials

were a week apart. Magdalen College in Oxford was always my first choice. I do wonder why, because many of my friends had gone to St John's College, Cambridge, where George Guest was the Director of Music. It was a choir of great singers which had a freedom very unlike the fussiness of King's, Cambridge. So the week before the Oxford auditions, I went up to audition in Cambridge for St John's.

Edred was good at making us choose an aria that showed us off. I was not a high tenor; I had difficulties with top As. So I found a beautiful aria, 'How vain is man' from Handel's oratorio *Judas Maccabeus*, which only goes up to an occasional top G. Nobody really sang that aria in those days. I remember the tenor who auditioned before me singing 'If with all your hearts' from Mendelssohn's *Elijah* and cracking on most of the top Gs. I also remember the organ scholar of St John's making a mess of the introduction to my aria, and it going through my mind that he'd be ticked off by George Guest afterwards. The next morning, I was just about to leave, and there was a knock on the door with a message from Guest, saying I shouldn't go to Oxford for the choral trials the following week, because he was offering me a choral scholarship to John's.

But I was very naive, and I went to Oxford the following week anyway. I went because it had been my first choice, and I subconsciously knew it was where I really wanted to go. I did the choral trials at Magdalen College, and had an interview with the Classics don, a delightful man called Colin Hardie. We didn't really talk about Classics, and he could see that my 'A' levels weren't any good, but he said, 'If you're successful in the choral trials I'll make sure you'll get a good degree.' And then for some reason I was also summoned over to do a choral trial at Christ Church. The organist there in those days was Simon Preston [celebrated English organist and conductor, organist at Christ Church from 1970 to 1981]. So I did what I was told: I had an interview with the Classics tutor at Christ Church, and it was unbearable. I was shaking like a leaf talking about Thucydides. He asked me why I wanted to come to Christ Church, and I told him I didn't, but he replied that Simon Preston wanted me. Anyway, I went home the next day and got a phone call from Bernard Rose at Magdalen College, Oxford.

*As in the composer Bernard Rose, who wrote the much-loved set of Anglican responses?*
Yes, the same. He said: 'I hear you want to go to St John's College, Cambridge.' I think he and George Guest were quite good friends and had discussed me. Bernard offered me a choral scholarship.

*So why was Magdalen, Oxford the place you wanted to go, rather than John's?*
When I look back on it, I must have known on some level that had I gone to Cambridge, I would have lived in the shadow of the likes of my King's Canterbury friends Stephen Barlow [conductor, principally of opera, married to Joanna Lumley] and Jonathan Sears [also an opera conductor]. They were good friends of mine, but were also musically and academically gifted. Jonathan went to John's, Cambridge and Stephen was already an organ scholar at Trinity, Cambridge.

*Were your parents supportive?*

My mother was the driving force in making me work. My father didn't say a lot, and because he had to look after the shop, he never came to hear me sing at Canterbury. My last day as a chorister at Canterbury was a Saturday. Services were 5 p.m. on a weekday but 3 p.m. on a Saturday, and poor Dad came over at 5 p.m. to see my last service and missed it by two hours. But he always kept a little picture of me as a chorister on the counter in the shop.

*So, did Oxford end up being the right place for you?*

Yes. I remember when Daniel Hyde [organist and conductor who was Music Director at Magdalen, Oxford, and succeeded Stephen Cleobury as Director of Music at King's College, Cambridge] went to Magdalen and I asked him how it was going, he said: 'I love Oxford, but there's no infrastructure for music like there is in Cambridge.' And I think that's what I liked about it: that there was no infrastructure. It's always been that way, and it gives you more freedom.

*What did your job as a choral scholar entail?*

We sang Evensong six days a week. It took place at six o'clock in the evening, as far as I remember, and we had to wait for the college bell to strike. Then we stood up and processed in. Bernard Rose loved programming an entire Evensong service of just one composer, for example Thomas Tomkins, or Kenneth Leighton.

Although I had been to public school before Oxford, I had been a day boy, so Magdalen was the first time I had really been away from home. The great thing about singing in the choir was that you landed straight into a community. You see these people every day of your life. I ran riot, being away from home – luckily I didn't go off the rails entirely, but I had a lot of fun. It was the 1970s, so there were student riots. In my first week, accommodation rents went up and the students protested by taking over the Examination Schools. I remember going to a disco in the Examination Schools in my second week there, with the police locked out. The head of the Junior Common Room in Magdalen was sent down for his political activities, and it was a major incident which hit the evening news. It was an exciting time to be there.

I was lucky with my friends, because they kept me on the straight and narrow. Of course, we had fun, but living in such close quarters meant that we learned to take care of one another. And it being the 1970s, we didn't have mobile phones, so we had almost no contact with home. I think I phoned home about twice a term, and my parents almost never came up to see me, so the chapel became my entire life. It was a wonderful community.

*Do you remember your rooms in Magdalen?*
Yes. As choral scholars we had rooms in college for all three or four years of our time there. In my first year, I had a room in St Swithun's Quad. It was very damp, on the ground floor, with a small bedroom at the back and a front room. It smelled musty. There was a damp patch on the wall and I bought a bit of material to cover it up, and made it my home. There was a young man living in the rooms above me who I think must have been a member of the Bullingdon

Club. He was a bit of a maniac, very wealthy, and got away with all sorts of things. There were people in college from all walks of life, with all kinds of political views, from the far right to the far left. There were students from state schools, from public school, wealthy, poor, fragile personalities and more, all living together under the one roof.

*What was the balance between your studies and your commitment to the chapel?*
I read Classics for the first two years, and my studies suffered. I had to miss quite a few seminars, because singing in chapel came first. We were singing different music every day of the week, and were expected to get it right. We all had keys to the song school, and we would let ourselves in every morning to check over the notes. Bernard Rose was brilliant, but we were quite scared of him, and we wanted to do a good job for him.

*What is the chapel itself like?*
It's a gorgeous building, and very intimate. Most of the chapels in Oxford are smaller than those in Cambridge. I think you can seat about 150 people in the stalls of Magdalen chapel, which isn't that many. The ante-chapel is almost bigger than the chapel itself. The two facing sides of the choir, which are known as *decani* and *cantoris*, sit very close to one another – you can almost shake hands across the aisle. In my day, the chapel was dark and quite dingy, and lit almost entirely by candles. As singers, we needed a bit more light, and we had a very clever contraption in our stalls: a real candlestick in a glass holder, at the bottom of which was a

small electric light to shine on our music. I think they were installed shortly before I arrived. But there was a flaw with them, because the electric light would get quite hot during the course of the service, and the candle above it would start to melt from the bottom up. Peter Nelson, the man responsible for the founding of The Sixteen, whom we will talk about later, was an architectural lighting designer, and because he loved Magdalen, he figured out a way to re-make them so that the candles didn't melt.

*And what was Bernard Rose like to sing for? You had been in these rather unusual Anglican environments that were somewhat freer than the norm. Was the atmosphere at Magdalen similarly free and maverick, or was it a bit of a culture shock for you?*
It was very different. I think I was a bit of a nuisance in the early days there – I'd keep talking about how they did things in Canterbury. But little by little, I started concentrating on my life in Oxford, and I made some very good friends. I sang in the choir for four years. I started off reading Classics and then switched to Music, so Bernard was also my tutor. When I think of it, the majority of choral scholars weren't music students. Bernard's speciality was Tudor church music, particularly the music of Thomas Tomkins, which we sang from his own editions, in handwritten script. He taught me how to cram as many bar lines as possible into a page of music when writing on manuscript paper. He'd get annoyed with his students who wasted space on the page. I remember there was one Tomkins anthem, *Almighty God, the Fountain of All Wisdom*, that was actually published by Schott's. It had a blue cover, and the pages inside were covered in Bernard's

red markings, replacing every one of the false relations that had been taken out. He was a skilled editor.

*Did that Tudor church repertoire resonate with you? Previously at Canterbury you'd sung under someone who didn't really 'get' Tudor music.*
Yes. I had gone up to Oxford loving Mahler and Franz Liszt, but the Tudor music I didn't really know. I was wary of it at first, but it didn't take long for me to realise what a joy it was. Bernard used to pose questions to his students, and invite questions too. If your answer was stupid, he'd never make you look a fool – he'd never make you look an idiot in front of your colleagues.

*What kind of questions?*
Oh, technical things like, 'Should that be an E natural or E flat?', or the underlay of the words.

*Had you previously been encouraged to talk about music in that way?*
No, that was a first. And we learned about the structure of the music through singing it.

*By the end of your four years at Magdalen, had you come to a decision that music was where you wanted your life to go?*
No, it still wasn't clear at all. I don't think many students come out of university actually knowing what they want to do. I certainly had no idea; but in those days, jobs were plentiful, and I went for all sorts of things. I went for a job as a research assistant at the British Museum, I got into the

music Hochschule in Hamburg, and I had ambitions to be a television producer, despite the fact I had no experience of television at all.

*But even though you didn't foresee a career in music, had something been sparked at Magdalen?*
Oh yes. I mean, I knew music would always be part of my life, that it would always be there, just perhaps as a sideline. I loved singing in a chapel choir, and singing different music every day. And I sang a lot outside chapel too. I sang in the early days of The Tallis Scholars, which was run by Peter Phillips, and I adored it. I also sang occasionally in David Wulstan's pioneering group, The Clerkes of Oxenford.

*When did you first come across David Wulstan?*
I saw him for the first time during my first term at Magdalen, even though I was reading Classics, and he wouldn't become my tutor for another two years when I switched to Music. In the Christmas of my first term, The Clerkes of Oxenford gave a concert in Magdalen chapel, and I remember it being packed to the rafters. I was blown away by the music, and this new and different sound. Peter Hayward, a friend of mine from Magdalen who was a countertenor, soon became a member of The Clerkes, so I would often go and listen to them.

When I switched my studies to Music, Wulstan was my music history tutor, and I found him a breath of fresh air. He knew about everything, and I hugely admired him. Still, it was something of a love–hate relationship. I came into the Music department not really knowing anything about it.

I remember my first tutorial with him. I had written an essay, and in those days we had to read our essays out loud to him. While I was reading, he fell asleep. If I had been a first-year student, I would probably have been too timid to say anything, but I was already a third-year, so I spoke up and asked him why he had fallen asleep. He told me that I had all but copied out *Music in the Baroque Era* by Manfred Bukofzer, the textbook of the day, which he claimed to know by heart even though he had never read it, because all of his students copied it out in their essays. He then challenged me to go away and think for myself. So the following week, I came back with an essay which was extremely critical of Bach's *St Matthew Passion*. I disliked Bach back then because I found his music so difficult to sing. Wulstan told me that although the content was nonsense, I had done a good job of thinking for myself.

*You don't still dislike Bach, do you?*
Oh no, of course I don't – I adore him. But I didn't come to love his music through singing it as much as through conducting it. I began to understand it more and more. Even so, I find that I have to work harder at interpreting Bach's music than I do Handel's.

Anyway, Wulstan was a big part of my time in Oxford. A lot of my friends sang in The Clerkes, as did I. I did enjoy it, but I so much more enjoyed the attitude of The Tallis Scholars. We were so cavalier about everything. We used to rate concerts using gin – the more difficult it was to sing the music, the more gin we would drink afterwards. We had so much fun. Having witnessed or been introduced to this music, one just wanted to do more and more of it. Peter felt that way. In fact, he worshipped The Clerkes. Wulstan introduced him to all this music, and from that moment onwards he knew that Tudor church music would be his life. I hadn't really got an idea of what I wanted to do, but when I did have the idea of forming a choir, I knew that I wanted to do it in a different way.

*And we'll pick up on that tomorrow. Before I go, can you give me a piece of music to listen to on the train down tomorrow? Something that relates to the next chapter of your early life: singing in Westminster Abbey, with the BBC Singers, and forming the earliest incarnation of The Sixteen.*

Why not something big, like Wylkynson's *Salve Regina*? It's the big showpiece of the Eton Choirbook, with some exquisite illuminations in the manuscript, and it has a great story behind it.

*I look forward to hearing it.*

## TWO
# Musical Beginnings
# (Part Two)

That evening, I listen to Wylkynson's *Salve Regina*, a remarkable piece of polyphony which appears on The Sixteen's *Pillars of Eternity* disc, Volume 3 of their survey of the Eton Choirbook. I take copious notes. But the next morning, at 7.30 a.m., Harry (who is clearly an early riser) emails me to change his mind. He would rather talk about another large-scale Tudor anthem, *Vox Patris caelestis* by William Mundy.

Mundy was a sixteenth-century composer, contemporary with Palestrina, and heavily influenced by Tallis and Sheppard. *Vox Patris* is an antiphon from around the same time as Palestrina's famous Mass, the *Missa Papae Marcelli*. The fact that it sets a Latin text suggests that it was written during the brief reign of the Catholic Queen Mary. It is on a vast scale, and elaborately written.

The Sixteen have recorded it twice: once for Hyperion in 1988 on a disc dedicated to Mundy's sacred music, and again for their own label, CORO, a disc called *The Voice of the Turtle Dove*. For an obscure piece of Tudor church music, it is relatively well known; The Tallis Scholars recorded it on their famous disc of the *Miserere* by Gregorio Allegri.

The journal *Early Music Review* said of The Sixteen's earlier recording that 'for a wallow in the richest cream of English Reformation church music, you couldn't do much better than this'. I find the recording, download it to my device, and listen on the train from Victoria.

The rain has cleared, and although the air has a late February chill and the sky leaving London is grey, the Kent countryside seems to unpack itself more proudly than yesterday. The train cuts through frenzied London construction sites south of the river and endless Victorian warehouses converted into storage facilities; for a moment, it tracks alongside the new Overground network, past the Victorian terraces of Wandsworth and Brixton, and then gradually emerges into the fresh air.

Like the landscape, Mundy's music unfolds slowly: at first, there are just two or three lines of counterpoint, but they soon blossom into a much richer texture as houses give way to scrub and rail sidings and, eventually, fields and horses. This is noble music, in which the text is of primary importance.

Harry meets me at the station once again, and drives me to the house, a mere five minutes away. He is being chivalrous; I am already eight months pregnant, and glad of any opportunity to sit. When we arrive at the house, he makes me tea and ushers me through to the conservatory. As I pass through the dining room, I notice a portrait of Harry lying flat on the table. It was painted by Ruth Fitton, who has been shortlisted by the Royal Society of Portrait Painters, and she needs it for her show, so it is due to be collected this afternoon. She captures Harry perfectly: dressed casually in jeans, sweater, scarf and woollen coat, he looks relaxed but engaged. His eyes sparkle. As in real life, he has an understated charisma.

As we sit down, Harry motions to a pile of sheet music sitting on the coffee table between us, and begins talking.

I've dug out some sheet music which I've kept since Oxford days, including the edition of *Almighty God* by Thomas Tomkins which I mentioned yesterday. It's covered in Bernard Rose's markings. You can see that he's changed the underlay of the text, and there's a lot of red ink where he's added in false relations, particularly in the 'Amen' at the end.

*How accurate is that? Is he returning the music to how it would have sounded, or rather saying that false relations are generally stylistically appropriate, and using that as licence to put in as many as he likes?*

The latter. He uses his own judgement about where the false relations might appear, according to the shape of a phrase. This symbol, which you can see appearing often, a dot surrounded by a circle, is what he used to call a 'short'. It was his own term for cutting short the last note of a phrase, usually making a crotchet into a quaver and taking a quaver rest. He would always mark it precisely in the score. I tend not to do that myself. There's no real reason for every voice to have to come off cleanly together in that way. I think it can sound fussy.

*Yes, I remember yesterday you spoke about the choral conductor's habit of being obsessed with the ends of phrases being tidy and perfect.*

I find it constricts the music. You spend all your attention on making the ends of phrases perfect, and not on trusting your singers to breathe. When I'm teaching the young singers in Genesis Sixteen, I talk about breath a lot. Take a Bach aria, for example. People often say Bach is difficult to sing because his music requires such long breaths, and he writes instrumentally for the voice. I suggest simply making the breath a part of the music, part of the phrase. There's no need to sing an entire eight-bar phrase without taking a breath. As a listener, it makes you feel breathless too.

*Today I would like to talk about the years you spent in London after Oxford, singing at Westminster Abbey and with the BBC Singers. Let's begin with the piece of music you've chosen to represent that transition. Yesterday you sent me off to listen to Wylkynson's* Salve Regina, *but this morning you changed your mind to William Mundy. We'll come onto Mundy in a moment, but tell me first why you picked the Wylkynson, which comes from the Eton Choirbook.*
I was thinking of the music I was introduced to in Oxford and found revelatory: those big, early antiphons. We sang them in The Tallis Scholars with Peter Phillips, who had either borrowed the scores from David Wulstan, or made his own handwritten editions. He would copy them out from the collected works of certain composers. They were incredibly complex pieces, and the challenge was always to get the notes in the right place.

*How readily available was this music at that time?*
There had been earlier editions of the Eton Choirbook by the likes of Frank Harrison in the 1950s, so there were certainly people who knew of the music before us, though perhaps not performing it in public. But in general it was rare.

The Eton Choirbook was compiled around 1500 for use in the chapel at Eton. There would have been chapels that had books like it all over the country, but because of the Reformation most of them were destroyed. It was only because of a miracle that the Eton Choirbook survived. It's thought that it was sent away to the bookbinders, because the leather was wearing away, and that's how it escaped. It wasn't found until 1895, and was discovered by the writer M. R. James, who was later to become Provost at Eton. He was cataloguing the library, and there it was, gathering dust on the bottom shelf. It contains numerous *Salve Regina* settings, and so much more. The composer most featured in it is John Browne, about whom we know nothing.

Wylkynson was, I think, the only composer in it connected to Eton – he was Master of the Choristers in the chapel there. What's interesting is that the two or three works by Wylkynson are in a different scribal hand to the rest of the book, quite likely his own. It's a massive partbook, and we know that this piece was sung more than any others because the parchment is worn away at the corners where the page has been turned over and over again. Fascinating. By the side of this piece, Wylkynson put all the hierarchy of angels – the archangels, cherubim . . .

*Oh, I see; each voice-part, instead of being labelled 'soprano', 'alto', 'tenor' and so on is labelled with a different category of celestial beings. That's unusual. And why did you pick this piece in particular?*

Partly because of the way it sounded when we sang it. David Wulstan originally started The Clerkes of Oxenford as an all-male group, but soon had the idea of adding women's voices to the top line. He had a theory that this repertoire would actually have been sung a minor third higher than notated, based in part on the pitch of organs from that period. He thought that the younger boys of Magdalen, Eton or Canterbury would have sung the highest parts, and the older boys whose voices were breaking would sing the mean line – the second line down. The countertenors would have an extremely large range from a B flat all the way down to the E flat or D below middle C. The tenor was the holding part, often singing a *cantus firmus*.

We sang this music stratospherically high, and it was a pioneering sound. It was ethereal, and it made people sit up and listen to repertoire they would otherwise have ignored. The sopranos singing those top lines were fearless, like Alison Stamp and Ruth Dean. It was liberating to sing this music that was new to all of us. It was fun and challenging at the same time. If we managed to get to the end of a piece without breaking down, that would count as a success, because they're incredibly long and hard works.

As I mentioned yesterday, I sang a bit with The Clerkes of Oxenford; I also sang with Peter Phillips' Tallis Scholars in their fledgling years; and when I left Oxford I just continued. When I started to put The Sixteen together with friends, it was in order to continue singing the music we had come to love. It was also for fun – we were cavalier about it. I don't know if groups can still do that today.

*Well, there are still many groups who form for the love of singing music together. Stile Antico, for example, were friends who loved exploring repertoire together. But I am curious what it is about this music that appealed to you. Tell me, for example, about the piece you chose for me this morning:* Vox Patris caelestis *by William Mundy. You've recorded it twice, the first time a minor third higher than printed, as you've described. It's a gigantic antiphon, like those pieces in the Eton Choirbook.*

It is, but interestingly it's much later. Most of the big fifteen-minute antiphons in the Eton Choirbook date from around the 1500s. But the Mundy is from around the reign of Queen Mary, some fifty years later. We know it dates from later partly because it's in Latin, and therefore Catholic. Nobody is quite clear why he wrote it, and academics like John Milsom have put forward various theories. One is that it was written for an outside event. There's an account of Queen Mary, on a pageant through London, stopping for a while and listening to a choir singing celestial, beautiful music. That's just one theory.

The piece has a similar structure to those other earlier pieces in the Eton Choirbook, but differs in that the lines are more vocal. Mundy has taken the archaic structure of the earlier pieces and created something sensual and evocative. The text is anonymous, a mixture of verses from the Song of Songs. For me, as a conductor, there's a great deal of room for interpretation. I think you can hear that if you just compare our two recordings of it. The earlier Eton Choirbook pieces are grand and rhythmically complex, which limits what you can do, but in Mundy there's a direction and drive to each verse, which you can do different things with in performance.

Later on in the piece, there is an extraordinary *gimmel*. A *gimmel* – as in twin – is where the parts divide. The soprano and alto lines split in two, and suddenly there is an ethereal passage on the word 'veni' – 'come my love', or 'arise my love'. It's incredibly sensual, and builds to the final, sumptuous 'Amen'.

I remember when we performed *Vox Patris* at a Choral Pilgrimage concert a few years ago, someone came up to me in the interval and said it was like listening to the slow movement of a Mahler symphony.

*When did you first come across it?*
With Peter Phillips, in the early days of The Tallis Scholars. His sound was based on a real purity in the top line, no vibrato at all, but the lower parts had more licence. I was one of only two tenors, and we had free reign to do what we liked. The group also contained what I call laser-beam altos: countertenors whose voices could cut through anything when singing up a minor third. Those voices don't really exist in the same way today. I'm thinking of people like David James, the countertenor who went on to shape the sound of The Hilliard Ensemble. David was a choral scholar before me at Magdalen, and sang in the early days of The Clerkes.

*Did you love that vocal quality of the laser-beam alto? I ask because I don't hear it in the sound of The Sixteen today. Yours is a totally different approach.*
Yes, today it is. But in the early days of The Sixteen I used voices like that. Peter Hayward, for example, whom I mentioned before, was a friend of mine who also sang with The Clerkes. He had a fantastic range, a more mellow sound, but

could cut through if he wanted. There were other extraordinary voices too, singing legends, who were part of The Sixteen for many years. I would always need that sound when we did the early repertoire at higher pitch. But I would also try to find another voice to balance it, to take the edge off the sound. Nowadays, if I made the group sing up a minor third, the sopranos would revolt.

*So, when did you change your approach, and stop putting pieces from that era up a minor third?*
Only a few years ago, really. I realised it was the wrong approach. Having said that, quite a few of those early discs for Hyperion that we made were all up a minor third, but by the time we get to the fifth volume of music by Sheppard or John Taverner I'd started taking it down a semitone, just to take the edge off for the sopranos.

*As a soprano myself, I'd like to thank you for that.*
I hesitated for so long because I thought that the music wouldn't be the same. Something like Sheppard's *Libera nos* was so beautiful with the sopranos soaring up to that top note, and I thought it would destroy it to bring the pitch down. But actually it's always going to be a great piece, and it takes on a completely different sonority. The altos end up singing higher, much more comfortably, and the tenors take over what were those grovelling alto parts. There's a different and much more pleasing texture, and I'm coming round to it. It's gradual – it took a long time – and I think Peter may still be doing pieces at the high pitch. John Milsom is one of my favourite musicologists, and he suggests performing at what-

ever pitch suits the singers in your choir. And who's to say what is authentic? These pieces were unaccompanied, so who knows where they got their note from? They could have done it at any pitch. But it is a fascinating sound-world, that music. With The Sixteen now, because we're doing such a range of other repertoire, when we do one of these big antiphons it takes us some time to get in the groove with it. But back in those days, it was much easier because it's all we were doing.

*Presumably for the conductor of a work like Mundy's* Vox Patris *– as with a Mahler slow movement – you're the one dealing with the architecture of the piece. The internal complexity, getting through it with all the notes in place, is the singer's job – but your job is to shape it, and give the whole journey meaning.* Yes, and that's particularly true of the Mundy. It's much later, and he writes more vocally, and there's more sense of line. With the earlier pieces in the Eton Choirbook, there's a limit to the word-painting; here it's much more obvious. If I'm dealing with one of those rhythmically complicated Eton Choirbook antiphons, I tend to look at those pieces vertically, whereas with a later piece like the Mundy I'm thinking of it horizontally, so there's more sense of shape to the overall piece. When you look further back to the music of Guillaume de Machaut or John Dunstable, you can see how music progressed to the excessive complexity of the 1500s, and then later things were different. Also, because the Mundy has such a sensual text from the Song of Songs, they're the most glorious words to get around. That's the beauty for the singers, making sure the vowels are enriched in the melismas, where one syllable is stretched over a long sequence of notes. All that music really depends on an ebb and flow.

If the Eton Choirbook composers had lived two centuries later, they would have been the Mozart, Brahms or Britten of their day. Back in the sixteenth century, the only employer for a musician was the church or the court, so that's who they wrote for. And back then, the music was subject to the liturgy. But one of the joys of those early days, with David Wulstan and Peter Phillips, was taking the music out and performing it to a growing public. And like with today's performances of Mozart, Brahms or Britten, the job of the conductor is to interpret the music.

Of course, one can be in danger of over-interpreting. If I find that what I'm doing sounds contrived, I forget it and go straight back to square one. When I was a young conductor, I loved George Malcolm's interpretation of the music of Victoria. I love Victoria's music, and I was obsessed by George Malcolm's recording of the *Tenebrae Responsories* with the choir of Westminster Cathedral. It was a captivating performance. Malcolm changed tempo left, right and centre, and his dynamics were wild, but it was gut-churning. And then I made the big mistake, when I came to conduct that music myself, of trying to copy Malcolm. It didn't work – it was a disaster, in fact – because it wasn't me. I learned quickly that you can't be inauthentic like that. I often notice the young conducting fellows on the Genesis Sixteen programme copying their favourite recordings, and I strongly discourage it.

*I want to come on to that another day, on to how you as a conductor find your authenticity, your voice. But let's carry on the*

*story first. You finished at Oxford, and had many possible avenues open to you, but you ended up singing at Westminster Abbey and then for the BBC Singers. How did that come about?*
Luck and chance.

*You always say that things happened just by chance – but at some point you must have known what you were up to.*
Oh, I don't know . . . I never did, really. I did four years at Oxford, and in my last year, because most of my friends had graduated, I worked hard and got a decent degree. One day, Bernard Rose came up to me and said he'd had a phone call from his friend Douglas Guest, organist at Westminster Abbey, saying they had a tenor vacancy. He asked if I would be interested in coming down to audition, and I said yes. I was, as usual, very casual about it. There were so many opportunities out there in general; life after university wasn't a worry like it is today. Consequently, we were very cavalier about it.

*I think most choral scholars leaving Oxbridge are cavalier even today. The choral scene in London is strong, and it's likely you'll find work deputising ('depping') for regular singers.*
Yes, I suppose they are.

*So how did your audition at the Abbey go?*
In a way, it was frightening. I had to sing plainsong from a green book. I hadn't ever had to sing plainsong like that before. Stephen Cleobury, who went on to spend several decades as Director of Music at King's College, Cambridge, was assistant organist, and he was very particular about how

things should be sung. I had to sing the second alto part of a fauxbourdon *Magnificat* down a fourth, or something complicated like that. But I rather enjoyed the experience, and I was offered a place.

So I made the move to London. I remember my first day at the Abbey. I only knew one singer there, David James. I wondered if I would get on with them all. But at the end of the first day, I asked if anybody wanted to join me in the pub, and off we all went. We had a great time, and I remember Richard Day-Lewis, one of the other lay clerks, giving me a word of advice: 'Wherever you go, take your diary and a pencil, because most of your work will come from going for a drink after a service.'

It was all so new to me. I had a salary for the first time – not much, but it made a difference. In fact, I had come out of Oxford having made a little bit of a profit; because my parents were shopkeepers, I had received the full grant from Wilson's Labour government. I shared a cheap flat in London with Peter Hayward, who had a job teaching at Holland Park School.

*So did the Abbey act as a springboard for the wider musical world?*
Yes, absolutely. Once I was at the Abbey, I started the process of auditioning for other things. My first audition, for John Eliot Gardiner and the Monteverdi Choir, didn't go well. I was very nervous, and it wasn't for me. It rather knocked my confidence. But the following week I sang for Richard Hickox, who in those days ran the Richard Hickox Singers. He also ran the music at St Margaret's Westminster, where

the audition was held. Richard was very kind, and although there wasn't a great deal of work, he put me on his list.

Shortly after that, I auditioned for English Music Theatre Company, the recently re-formed English Opera Group, which Britten had started. Steuart Bedford, who ran it, auditioned me in his flat in Maida Vale. Steuart was a legend even then; he had gained a First at Oxford, and the story went that they kept him back for an hour or more at his *viva*, giving him score after score to sight-read, expecting him to make a mistake – but he never did. He was also Britten's disciple, and I was in awe of him. I brought along the first of Britten's five Canticles, *My Beloved is Mine*, to sing, and Steuart played for me, which was quite a thrill. He offered me a place in the chorus, and that got me into opera.

My first professional opera job was singing Third Gondolier in Britten's *Death in Venice* at the Royal Opera House. Britten's partner and muse Peter Pears was singing, of course, and as a tenor he was my idol. I had sung in his presence once before; my first special service at Westminster Abbey, in November 1977, was Britten's memorial service, one year after his death. It felt to me as though things were coming full circle: having sung in Britten's *Noye's Fludde* at choir school and been introduced to Britten's music as a boy, I was now singing at Covent Garden with Peter Pears. It was an honour to be part of that ensemble. The production was by Colin Graham, and the cast included John Shirley-Quirk and James Bowman. Steuart Bedford conducted in such a way that I could understand every note that Britten wrote in his scores. We revived the production at Aldeburgh a year or two later, which was to be the last time Pears sang the role of

Aschenbach before the first of his strokes. I remember that he was very nervous at Covent Garden, but when it came to Aldeburgh he was incredibly relaxed, and got every note right. We also performed Britten's *Paul Bunyan*, and I was one of the four Swedes. Richard Suart was another – we had a hilarious time, wearing blond wigs. I was delighted to be earning money doing what I loved.

Unfortunately, the Arts Council cut the funding for English Music Theatre Company, and it came to an end. The last thing we did was at the Old Vic, an inspiring work by the Japanese composer Minoru Miki, with a blend of classical and Eastern instruments. I was extremely sad when the group ended. I was in it for about three years, from 1978. For each of those productions, I was away from the Abbey, but still employed by them, and around the same time I also got onto the *ad hoc* list for the BBC Singers.

*Who directed the BBC Singers in those days?*
John Poole. As today, the BBC Singers was the only professional full-time choir in the country, and it was a dream for any singer to get on their *ad hoc* list. The fees were good, they offered a lot of work, and I was lucky to get on the list straight away after my audition.

The audition itself was bizarre. It took place in the Radio Theatre, in the basement of BBC Broadcasting House, where lunchtime recitals were held. I had to start by singing a set-piece aria, something like 'Ev'ry valley' from Handel's *Messiah*. For the whole audition, I was alone in the room; John Poole and Geoffrey Mitchell (the BBC Singers' general manager) were hidden in the control box, talking to me over a loudspeaker. John told me to walk over to the piano and pick up one of the numerous pieces of sheet music sitting there, and sight-read. It began with music by Bach, then Hugo Wolf, Kenneth Leighton, then Anton Webern – progressively harder. And then the voice said, 'Please sing an arpeggio starting on a bottom C.' I remember singing as high up the arpeggio as possible. That was the first – and the last – top C I ever sang in my life. Because I had sung so high, John put me on first tenor, and once I was in the group I had to explain to him that I actually had a slightly lower voice than he thought.

*What was John like to sing for?*
I loved John. He had his critics; he had a loose way of conducting, and he didn't much like rehearsing. Often, the more difficult a piece was, the less he'd rehearse it. In the first couple of months of the year, we would sing a lot of very tricky contemporary music, which is where the sight-reading skills from the audition came in useful. They were usually conducted by John's assistant conductors, such as Nicholas Cleobury.

And meanwhile, day in day out I was singing at Westminster Abbey. I stood next to David James for all of that, and I had an older tenor on my other side who was a very reliable singer. Today it's so much more professional there. In my day there was a lot more messing around. I remember the first time I had to sing a solo in a verse in the canticles. It was Harwood's *Magnificat* in A flat, with a tenor solo that goes all the way up to a top A flat. I was gearing myself up to this verse, and just before it David James took my copy and threw it to one side. So I was quick on my feet, and grabbed the copy off the tenor to my left. But then just as I started to sing David poked me in the back, and I belted out the A flat. I've never laughed so much as in those days.

In many ways, I was continuing to be a student, and being paid for it: having fun, laughing a lot, being a bit of a hooligan – and that's never quite left me. That's part of why The Sixteen has continued as long as it has, because we have so much fun together. We have fun in our concerts too, and there's nothing wrong with that.

*So how did your career as a conductor begin?*
My thoughts of being a professional singer began to dwindle with the collapse of English Music Theatre Company. So in 1982, after five years, I resigned from Westminster Abbey. In January 1983, I had a phone call from Geoffrey Mitchell at the BBC Singers offering me a permanent place in the group; until then, I had been on their *ad hoc* list. At first, I turned it down, because I wanted to focus on conducting and developing The Sixteen. But John Poole rang me later the same day, and offered me the job again. He pointed out that I had to live – I had just got married and taken on a mortgage – and that the Singers would support me with every bit of conducting I wanted to do, by letting me off rehearsals and concerts. I accepted the job, and for three years I was a member of the BBC Singers. It was one of the best things for me, because I had paid work at the same time as getting The Sixteen going.

Being a permanent member of the BBC Singers taught me so much. The big plus side was working with conductors like Pierre Boulez, Seiji Ozawa and Gennady Rozhdestven-sky. We recorded all of Arnold Schoenberg's male-voice songs with Boulez. Schoenberg himself had said they were unperformable, and they had never been recorded before. Boulez adored the BBC Singers, and we continued to be irreverent when we worked with him: I remember someone bringing a whoopee cushion to a rehearsal, and Boulez laughing along with us. We also performed Boulez's own music. The first time we read through a piece, I would find it really hard, but he would talk us through it, and it suddenly became clear. He would explain the text, and why he had used particular orchestral colours, and once it was illuminated like that, I found it to be such expressive music. I think Boulez was more like Messiaen than he would have admitted, particularly in terms of texture, colour and the way he utilised the instruments of the orchestra.

As a conductor, he didn't use a baton, and he did what's known as 'mirror-beating', a rather wooden style where the left and right hands do the same thing in mirror image. Most of his music was in complex time signatures, like 22/16, but he was incredibly clear and amazingly expressive for it. Not only his hands were expressive: his face was too. It didn't say much, but what it did say was so communicative.

Rozhdestvensky, unlike Boulez, hated rehearsing. On the day of Charles and Diana's wedding in 1981, we performed at the BBC Proms. It was a programme of Igor Stravinsky's *Les Noces* and *The Rite of Spring*, with Rozhdestvensky conducting the BBC Symphony Orchestra and Singers. I stayed behind at our rehearsals to hear my idol conducting *The Rite of Spring*. He got halfway through the bassoon solo at the start, and stopped the rehearsal, simply saying: 'tomorrow'. The leader of the orchestra looked ashen-faced. The following day, I stayed behind again to hear more. He got three bars beyond the bassoon solo, and stopped again, saying: 'tonight'. The leader protested, because the orchestra had to rehearse – it had been some time since they'd performed the piece in concert. But Rozhdestvensky simply said: 'I know this piece.' The performance was the most electric I've heard in my life. Rozhdestvensky was an extrovert. He had a baton nearly two feet long. Once, we were doing a piece of contemporary music, and the violas, after about eighty-two bars rest, came in on a high and piercing trill. Just before their entry, he leaned back, pulled back the baton, and flicked it like a bow and arrow as the trill started. What a showman!

And then there was Seiji Ozawa. I particularly remember performing Acts 1 and 2 of Messiaen's *St Francis of Assisi* with him. Messiaen hadn't completed it at that point. We performed with the BBC Symphony Orchestra in London, and then went over to Berlin to do it with the Berlin Philharmonic. Ozawa adored the Singers, and Messiaen was there in rehearsals, writing bits as we went along. Ozawa conducted everything from memory. I always have the score with me, myself, because if I can see it, something different occurs to me every time I conduct a piece. But Ozawa was sensational. He had the whole score from memory, except for two little bits of photocopied paper which Messiaen had inserted during the rehearsals.

I learned so much from working with that calibre of conductor, and watching how they worked. Of course, I also learned from conductors we worked with who didn't know how to rehearse well, and those lessons have stayed with me too.

*What a rich and varied musical diet you had then. You were singing Tudor polyphony with The Tallis Scholars, and at the same time Messiaen and Boulez with the composers themselves present. You strike me as someone with a broad musical appreciation, but was there any repertoire you were reluctant to perform?*
Not really. I did have a little black book, when I was in the BBC Singers, which I've sadly lost. But in the front of the book, I wrote down the pieces of music we sang which I wanted to conduct myself one day; and in the back, I wrote down the few pieces I never wanted to do again.

The works I wanted to conduct myself included Francis Poulenc's *Figure humaine*; Hans Werner Henze's *Orpheus Behind the Wire*; Giles Swayne's *Cry*, which we performed at the BBC Proms with twenty-six individually miked voices, and Steve Reich's *Desert Music,* which we did with conductor Peter Eötvös. These works were a revelation to me.

*And what about the pieces you didn't like?*
Mainly, they were pieces where I felt the text wasn't clear. There seemed to be a fad in the 1980s for scattering syllables of text throughout the vocal parts, and it often led to a lack of clarity. There were a few individual pieces by composers such as David Bedford, Alexander Goehr or Hugh Wood, whom I otherwise admired greatly, which I found hard to take. But in general, I was very open to most of the music we were performing. I loved Peter Maxwell Davies' music, Harrison Birtwistle, Edward Cowie, Giles Swayne and many

more besides. I am always willing to be challenged, as I was with Birtwistle's *Gawain*, for example – but the challenge has to be worthwhile in the end.

But the music I really loved was the Renaissance repertoire, which I was singing at Westminster Abbey and with The Tallis Scholars. In both cases, I felt frustrated because I wanted to get behind these works in a different way, interpret them, and not just sing the notes on the page in the right order, in tune and with a nice sound. So during that time, The Sixteen evolved. The more I thought about it, the more I realised it came down to the words. The composers in the Eton Choirbook were inspired by text. Whenever I look at a piece of music for the first time, I look at the text, and I try to get as close to it as possible. I formulate my approach to the music based on the text.

*So tell me about the beginnings of The Sixteen. It didn't happen overnight, but where did the story start?*
It began straight after I left Oxford and went to the Abbey, not quite knowing what I wanted to do. In fact, at the time, my mother decided she wanted me to be a singer, and put me in for every competition; they would come through the letterbox and I never opened them, just put them in a pile. When I eventually told her I wanted to conduct, she was mortified.

*When did you know you wanted to conduct?*
From quite early on. I did a bit of conducting at Magdalen, putting on the odd concert, and I enjoyed it. Bernard Rose was really useful, he taught me to start with a click in the beat. You watch Valery Gergiev, the celebrated Russian conductor,

and wonder what's happening because his fingers flutter all over the place, but there's a click somewhere in there.

I had met a man at Magdalen called Peter Nelson. He ran an architectural lighting business in Reading and sorted out the lights in the chapel, and he used to come regularly to Evensong. He loved the choir, and when I and my contemporaries left, he asked me to come back and put on a concert for him. He was a one-off; he had long grey hair, drove a beaten-up Land Rover, and thought that music stopped at about the year 1670. He paid for the concert: Gibbons verse anthems, Pelham Humfrey – late Tudor music from the Chapel Royal. I put together the choir, which consisted of one or two colleagues from Oxford; some from my Canterbury days like Duncan Perkins, with his beautiful oak bass voice; Nick Robertson, who'd gone to Cambridge from Dover College; and others I had met through The Clerkes of Oxenford. All the altos were male, and the soprano line female. First and foremost, the singers I chose were all friends.

*And apart from them being your friends, can you tell as you look back on that original line-up why you brought that particular group of voices together?*

Yes. It's because they were different characters and personalities. Everyone brought something different to the group. A high percentage were from a similar culture – those who'd been through The Clerkes or The Tallis Scholars – but there were others who weren't. They were singers with fantastic diction and phrasing, which was important to me because of my interest in the text.

[ 63 ]

*Was the concert a success?*
Yes, and Peter kept asking me to do them – we did two or three a year. At first, we weren't paying the choir, except with beer, and later on we offered a fee of £10.

*And did you immediately become The Sixteen?*
Well, having done these concerts, we needed to decide on the group's name. Somebody suggested The Sixteen, since we were doing sixteenth-century music and there were six-teen of us, and we settled on that. And then Peter decided to pay for us to do a London concert at St John's Smith Square, in May 1979. We had a run-in concert in Magdalen first, a chance to try out the same programme, which included Mundy's *Vox Patris caelestis*. I suppose at that point I felt I had something to say with that piece, that music in general: not just make a beautiful sound, but make the words live a bit more. The rehearsal was in the morning, because the FA Cup Final (Arsenal vs Manchester United) was in the afternoon, and Arsenal, my team, won. We bombed down to Richard Price's place in Catford to watch the final, and then came back to do the concert. I put an Arsenal rosette on the back of my music stand, so the sing-ers could see it.

The concert was reviewed in *The Times*, and although I've lost the cutting, I remember it said that not only was the sound of the choir a revelation, so was the music itself. And it was at that point that I began to think: this is what I really want to do.

In 1981 came another turning point, because Hugh Keyte, then a BBC producer, came to hear us, and invited us to do a

BBC lunchtime concert. We were the only choir other than the BBC Singers to give one of those lunchtime concerts. I think we did Mundy's *Vox Patris caelestis* then too. At a time when The Tallis Scholars were starting to go strong, it's strange that Hugh asked us first. He obviously heard something in us that he liked. He then booked some sessions for us, in which we recorded some of the Chapel Royal anthems.

*So at what point did The Sixteen become so established that you could let go of these other jobs?*

Throughout that time I realised I wanted to take The Sixteen further. One thing that made a huge difference was our first recording. I invited Ted Perry to a concert. Ted was the founder of Hyperion Records, but at that point was running something called Meridian Records with John Shuttleworth. I got chatting to him at the concert, and realised it was John and not Ted I was talking to, so we started recording with Meridian. And then later we moved to Hyperion with Ted.

At the same time, we started working with the music agency Magenta Music, run by John Bickley and Paul James. They took us under their wing. Their main client was The Hilliard Ensemble, and they represented a lot of up-and-coming early-music singers. They felt that the only way The Sixteen could generate income was to work for other people. For three years, we were the opera chorus of the Aix-en-Provence Festival, and we also started working with Ton Koopman as the choir for his Amsterdam Baroque Orchestra. That collaboration lasted a couple of years, and included performances of Bach's B minor Mass and *St*

*Matthew Passion.* I learned a lot from Ton – he was full of musical ideas and passion – but I began to feel more and more that I wanted to do things my way. So, instead, I formed my own orchestra to perform with The Sixteen.

Separately to The Sixteen, John also managed to get me conducting jobs, not with other choirs, but with orchestras. I realised that if I wanted to conduct, I had to be able to conduct an orchestra as well. I hadn't gone to music college, or trained as a conductor, and my whole style had developed simply by watching others like Boulez and Rozhdestvensky, seeing the rhythm in their bodies and expression in their faces. I was lucky to have opportunities to learn and make mistakes, and that it happened away from England. I worked with the Deutsche Kammerphilharmonie Bremen, Tapiola Sinfonietta, and Avanti!, the chamber orchestra started by Esa-Pekka Salonen and Jukka-Pekka Saraste. A couple of years later I conducted an opera in Lisbon. But I made a point of not conducting any choirs other than The Sixteen.

I was so lucky to have all of these things running simultaneously. It gave me the confidence to give up singing altogether, and focus on conducting and founding The Sixteen. I could follow my love of doing what I enjoyed, something that stemmed right back to my days in Canterbury, making music for the sheer enjoyment of it. And the wonderful thing about having your own group is that you can reflect your own taste in music. Of course, there is music I love that I don't get to conduct.

*Such as?*

Mahler. I love Mahler, but you'll never hear me conduct his music – I'll leave that to others.

*Never say never, Harry.*

## THREE
# The Sound of The Sixteen

The English have a charming habit of naming nature in a vain attempt to tame it. Today, the 'Beast from the East', an Arctic weather front from Russia, is spiralling its way down the east coast of England, peppering London with snow.

Before I leave home for Kent, I listen to The Sixteen's sumptuous 1990 recording of Francis Poulenc's *Figure humaine*, one of the pieces Harry had noted down in his little black book. This wartime cantata for double choir, which sets poems by Paul Éluard (whom Poulenc knew), makes for a bracing start to the day. There is almost no counterpoint in the music. Instead, Poulenc renders the terror and tenderness of Éluard's poetry in constantly shifting floes of harmony, at times quicksilver in their execution, at others like giant slabs of marble.

The snow has caused predictable travel chaos, but the train leaves on time, and I listen again on headphones. The music is harmonically busy, but as I look out over Kentish fields dappled with powdery snow, my attention is drawn to what seems like a great, white silence at the heart of it.

The eighth and final song, 'Liberté', acts as an epilogue to the cantata, and is laden with significance. During the war, the British Royal Air Force dropped Éluard's poem, printed on leaflets, all over occupied France, to encourage the Resistance and lift morale. Poulenc's setting begins simply, with short, delicate phrases. Each syllable lands on a different harmony, led by a soprano line of fragmented half-tunes, more plainsong than melody. As we approach Otford station, the movement slows to a triumphant halt, a richly satisfying cadence on the word *liberté*, and, quite unexpectedly, the last soprano note takes flight to a high E in an almost-scream of defiance.

Harry meets me at the train station, and we drive up to the house. Saffie, the family's dog, is in seventh heaven, diving her face hungrily into fresh piles of snow. As we sit and talk, we are interrupted every so often by her whitened beard bounding past the conservatory windows.

Today, our conversation turns to the sound of The Sixteen: how it has changed over the years, born of the early-music movement but also very much in resistance to its purity; the timbre of the group, and Harry's focus on text; how he chooses singers and personalities, and how he lets the music lead the sound. We finish at the Choral Pilgrimage, to pick up there the following day.

৵

*Let's begin with Poulenc's* Figure humaine. *When did you first encounter it?*
I first sang it in the BBC Singers, and I knew immediately I wanted to conduct it. I hadn't come across much Poulenc at university, aside from the occasional motet. I remember a certain recording we made with the BBC Singers of the Christmas or Lenten motets, and the conductor spoke of how Poulenc is very specific in his scores, and one should obey them strictly – for example, if he doesn't write in '*rallentando*',

you mustn't ever slow down at the end of a phrase. I was struck by how wooden the music sounded as a result – it didn't breathe.

Over the years I've come to realise that, because of Poulenc's deep faith, his music is always a personal expression of the text. *Figure humaine* isn't a religious work, but it has a powerful story and meaning. Éluard's poetry is about the savagery of conflict. The score was smuggled to Belgium from occupied France, and published there first in private. On the day the Allies liberated Paris, Poulenc threw open his window and placed the score of *Figure humaine* there for all to see – his version of hanging a *tricolore* flag out of his window. The last poem, 'Liberté', was really the bible of the Resistance.

The Sixteen recorded *Figure humaine* in Snape Maltings in 1989, the early days of Virgin Classics. We arrived the evening before we started recording, and the Suffolk countryside was peaceful. But when we woke the next morning, there was mayhem in the air: jets flying over from the American airbase next door. We immediately turned on BBC Radio 4 to find out what was happening, and discovered that Ronald Reagan's administration had shot down two Libyan planes. Nobody knew what would happen. The producer for Virgin phoned the main office in London, who in turn phoned the American airbase, and told them we were trying to make a recording. It was extraordinary, really, that we were about to record a work written during the Resistance, while there was a possibility of war around us. The Americans did a security check on all the singers, and then just before lunchtime, a motorbike arrived to deliver a folder, in which was a complete schedule of all the jets that would be flying over that day, so that we could organise our sessions around them. We had to record in five-minute segments, each one in total concentration.

*That must have been desperately frustrating, but I imagine that* Figure humaine *is one of the few works it's actually possible to record in tiny segments like that. Everything is in fragments, short plainsong-like phrases, slabs of harmony.*
Yes, it's one of the characteristics of Poulenc's music. But it leads to a common mistake people make performing his music; it is homophonic, written in block harmonies, but you have to allow it to breathe. You have to have a French coach, right from the start, at the same time as you learn the notes. Poulenc was an accomplished pianist and I imagine wrote a lot of it at the piano, but he was also a great master of writing a tune, he knew how to write for the voice. Once you find a way through the intervals, it all starts to make sense.

*What is the way in?*
Through the words, and through listening intently to the chords and paying attention to how to balance them. Above all, getting the shape of the French vowels. English singers are notoriously lazy. In French, the mouth shapes for vowels are different from those in English. We worked really hard at it. Because the piece is so monumental, there wasn't a single singer in the group who didn't want to accept the challenge, or who didn't get great enjoyment out of it.

We've just been doing a Genesis Sixteen weekend, and our young conducting fellow did 'Timor et tremens', the first of Poulenc's Lenten motets, his *Quatre motets pour un temps de pénitence*. He was allowing the music to be regimented by the bar lines, which made it sound rigid. But the word stresses aren't necessarily on the bar line, and I had to encourage him not to be metronomic or regimented. The music follows the natural inflections of the language. When singers get that, the music suddenly takes shape.

*Do you make your singers speak through the text first?*
Yes. Not always with The Sixteen anymore, but certainly with the Genesis Sixteen younger singers, and also quite often with the Handel and Haydn Society in Boston. It all goes back to Monteverdi: sing as you speak. It doesn't matter what the music is – a Finzi part-song, an anthem by Byrd, Purcell – the basic principles are the same, and if you inflect the words properly, you're halfway there.

*I was listening to the 1990* Figure humaine *release, and I can tell it's The Sixteen. I've been trying to pinpoint what the qualities are that make your group so recognisable. Have you always had a clear sense of the sound you wanted to create with The Sixteen, regardless of repertoire?*
That's difficult to answer. I think there are two things – the music we sing and the people who sing it. Part of it is the way we started, with sixteenth-century English music, which we sang right from the inception of the group through all the discs we recorded for Hyperion, all through the 1980s. When you look back at that discography, all the repertoire is by Tallis, Sheppard, Mundy, Taverner and Robert Fayrfax. So I was shaping the sound from inside that repertoire, even if it has a consistency across all kinds of music.

[ 72 ]

*How has the sound of the group changed over the years?*
I would say that it has matured over the years rather than changed radically. That maturity has partly to do with the singers. We have the older singers who have been with me for a long time, who know what I want, and the younger singers who learn how to adopt that style from the older ones. The personnel of the group has always changed, but it has become more stable since 2000. Throughout the 1980s, I tended to use one group of singers for the recordings and the *a cappella* concerts, and another group of singers who did the projects with orchestra. Although there was always a nucleus of people who stayed the same, there was more fluidity when it came to the singers.

The sound of the group certainly developed through the 1990s when we made all those recordings. But even listening to our earliest recordings, I can still hear the basic principle of the group's sound: allowing freedom for the singers. Another reason for the sound's maturity is the quality of singers. We have always had excellent singers in the group, but it's like athletes. Somebody breaks a world record, and you can't imagine anyone being faster, but twenty years later the records keep on being broken. It's the same with singers – the standard just gets better and better as time goes on. And people are more professional too, taking care of their voices. Back in the early days, singers would go to the pub before a concert. That would never happen today. Performers are much more aware of what they are doing. They realise that they have to perform to the very best of their abilities whether we are singing for an audience of twenty people or two thousand.

One constant characteristic of the group is that there have always been excellent voices. In the early days, I was fixing the singers in the choir myself; more recently I've had someone in the office doing the fixing. But in both cases we are concerned with making sure the voices and personalities work well together. The singers have to support the person standing next to them and also feed off them. I want people to sing with their natural voice, and not sing for me how they think the music should go. I don't want someone predicting what I want. If I can hear their natural voice, I can then work with that. More often than not, I say to people I want more warmth in the sound.

*That makes sense, because I would describe the sound of The Sixteen as warm.*
Yes, but people also say the sound is very pure.

*Well, it's the combination of the two. When you mention the early repertoire you sang – Sheppard, Mundy, Taverner – that's the same repertoire The Tallis Scholars were singing, but they sound completely different. What seems to mark your group out as different is the warmth of your sound, the depth and richness of the sonority. Does that come from the fact you're encouraging your singers to sing out, and use the full timbral range of their voices?*
Yes, but it's not a question of volume, to be clear. Singing out can sometimes mean singing loudly, which can also restrict the voice. Restricting the voice will lead to someone either singing off the voice, or the soft palate will collapse so you lose the resonance. I want to hear a real blade in the

sound, and the voices constantly spinning the sound so that the vowels are never dull.

*Why do singers in the UK grow up restricting their voices – is it the choral training?*
Yes. Conductors or choirmasters often say they want a 'straight sound'. The first response is to tighten.

*By straight sound, you mean without vibrato?*
Exactly. It's all about mimicking the boy treble. In the treble voice there's not a great amount of vibrato. The trouble is, vibrato has come to be seen as a 'sin' – and it's not. It's a baroque expression for warmth. When vibrato gets out of hand, which often happens with young singers, where it waves around – that's not real vibrato, that's just bad technique, and you have to kill that immediately. Vibrato, when it works, gives a warmth and richness or halo to the sound, and helps it to carry.

I remember once we were recording music by Victoria, and one of the singers with a very early-music voice was giving us the notes to start on. He had perfect pitch and no vibrato at all, and it was impossible to tell what note he was singing; consequently, our tuning was all over the place. The voice needs the bloom of vibrato to communicate the tonality of the note.

Of course, there's a type of music, such as Machaut, that needs that straightness of sound. But I think things went too far in the early-music movement, conductors asking for no vibrato at all, rather than just a slightly straighter sound. As soon as singers are given the command 'no vibrato', they tighten up and constrict their natural voice. I'll sometimes use a straighter sound to get a special effect, but the norm is always warmth. Thinking from the early days, when we did Sheppard and so on, it was a reaction to what I'd been hearing at Oxford in those days, that excessive purity of sound, which was beautiful but sexless, and I wanted more sensuality in the sound.

It also has to do with how we look at early music. For me, too many people out there just attach a syllable to a note, so there's no sense of phrase. On our most recent course with Genesis Sixteen we were doing a *Nesciens mater* setting from the Eton Choirbook – quite a short piece, and very rhythmic. The singers had the music in advance. Quite a few of them had come from conservatoires, where perhaps the sight-reading isn't as good as in university chapel choirs. The Friday rehearsal was dire, they were fighting the rhythms and couldn't get round the notes; the ensemble was terrible. So I told them that with a lot of this music you need to think either vertically or horizontally. For quite a few sections of this piece they needed to think vertically, treat the rhythms as funky – and bit by bit we got it together. And then I asked them to use the geography or the contour of the line of the music, and phrase accordingly. I think it was Bernard Rose who told me that right up until Beethoven, music had been based on architectural forms, such as proscenium arches, or the structure of cathedrals. If you think in those arches and contours then things make sense. You have to find a line through the phrase. I don't tell them where to breathe or how to articulate it – they need to find that for themselves. There was one phrase they were all singing horribly. I told them to think of the piece of music, and imagine that at the top of the manuscript it said 'Richard Strauss'. And it sounded absolutely beautiful. It sounded like a piece of music. By the end, they had really got it.

*That shift from purity to warmth, back in those early days, must have been tremendously exciting. You'd grown up in a particular tradition, surrounded by a rather purist approach in your contemporaries, so it must have felt good to find a new voice.*
It was, but it took a long time, it was a gradual process. I knew at university when I sang these pieces that, for me, there was something missing – we were taking it out of its liturgical context, bringing it into a concert hall, and we had to be doing something more than just singing the notes. If we think this music is good we have to be treating it as music to perform for a public. If those composers had lived two hundred years later, they'd have been writing operas.

*By performing that liturgical music in a concert hall, you're immediately acknowledging the paradox at the heart of the authenticity movement. As people in the twentieth and twenty-first centuries, performing in concert halls, we can't ever hope to replicate or indeed know what this music actually sounded like.*
I think that's true. People often describe The Sixteen as a period or authentic music group, but that's wrong. To begin with, we have always had women singing the top line of music, which is by no means authentic. And today, I encourage my sopranos to sound like sopranos. In contrast, David Wulstan wanted the female singers of The Clerkes of

Oxenford to emulate the sound of boy trebles, who would have sung that music originally. He would allow the men to do what they liked, but ask the women to sing in an unnatural way. When I realised that wasn't their natural way of singing, I moved away from it with The Sixteen. Of course, I have used sopranos who can sing incredibly high with great ease, like Carolyn Sampson, but she has real warmth and character in her voice too. I needed a soprano line that was warm and not boyish, to balance out the sound of the male altos, who were necessary because of the higher pitch at which we were singing this repertoire.

So, forming the sound of The Sixteen was a gradual process of allowing people to sing, and of getting to know the style of the sixteenth-century repertoire. At the same time, because we were taking this liturgical music out of context by moving it into the concert hall, we had to pay even more attention to the text. Most of it is in Latin, and our audiences – unlike those who would have heard it as part of the liturgy – didn't speak any Latin. So we had to make the words come to life. Even if we were performing part of the well-known Mass, we still had to get those words and their meaning across to our listeners.

One of my greatest challenges in those early days was learning not to over-interpret the music for the concert hall. I so wanted to put my personal stamp on it. I mentioned in our earlier conversation about having been obsessed by George Malcolm's recording of Victoria's *Tenebrae Responsories*; I learned from that experience that I needed to find my own way into the music. In fact, I also learned that from David Wulstan. He taught me to think for myself, both in writing essays and in conducting. If what I was doing sounded contrived, I'd go back to square one, because ultimately I wanted to make this music sound natural and organic, so that its beauty, majesty and emotion could come through.

*You just mentioned Carolyn Sampson, one of the many wonderful singers you've had in the group. I'm interested in the part individual voices play in shaping the sound of The Sixteen. On the one hand, you talk about individual voices; on the other hand, you achieve a coherent sound with those individuals. I certainly never hear voices sticking out of the texture in your recordings. They always blend well. Tell me about choosing your singers.*

Well, I'm very loyal to my singers. I've often said that someone is either there for one concert, or they're there for ten years. You know pretty quickly if someone is going to work. Everybody who has sung for the group has a good voice, but I'm more interested in the way they relate to one another, their body language, and the way they listen. I need singers to listen, not to be blinkered in their own parts, but to have a constant awareness of what's happening in the other parts. And I need them to be humble. If you're singing in a section with three other tenors, you have to work with them and feed off them. Certain singers are particularly good at feeding off others. The timbre of the individual voices can be varied, but because of the way they sing with each other they sound cohesive. Take Jeremy White, for example, who has a magnificent bass voice. He's now on the staff at Covent Garden. His voice is immense, and it gave a fantastic sonority to the bass line. At the same time, we had the tenor Nick Robertson, who had a wild voice that often needed taming, but was so musical and knew exactly how I wanted the music shaped. There's also a balance between ages. The older singers are put on their mettle by the presence of talented young singers, while the younger ones learn a huge amount from the older ones. And I tend to be able to tell pretty quickly, from just one rehearsal, if someone's character will work with the rest of the singers in the group at the time. Mostly it's about body language. Sometimes, you come across a singer who is disruptive, either socially or musically. It might be that they're not adaptable, or that their tuning is wayward, or their vowel sounds are one-dimensional and it's clear they can't be changed.

*So how do you find singers, and choose them for the group?*
It's always word of mouth. In the early days, I used people I encountered through singing myself, or went by recommendations. Often they were younger singers coming down from Oxbridge. I wouldn't usually book the ones who were very fine and off to music college, those clearly destined for something very good quite quickly, because I wanted people who would stick with the group.

*But you've had some pretty starry names coming through the group, nevertheless.*
Yes. The tenor Mark Padmore joined us straight after university, and stayed for about ten years. Then he came to a decision that he wanted to have a go at a solo career, and he stopped choral singing altogether, and I fully supported him. There was always a place for him in the group if it didn't work out. The bass Christopher Purves is another.

They had great voices and personalities too, real character. I also remember hearing Carolyn Sampson for the first time. She was just about to leave university, and I immediately knew I wanted her in the group, that her voice would be something special. Those singers have all made a decision to go on to a solo career, despite the fact that it would be more lonely than singing in a choir.

I invited Christopher Purves to come and speak on our latest Genesis Sixteen course, and he said something wonderful: that singing in The Sixteen for him was all about three Fs: fun, friendship and forgiveness. He said that these days, when he sings in an opera, it's rare that the whole cast gets on as well as The Sixteen's singers always did. We've spoken about fun and friendship already, but forgiveness is very important too. If someone makes a mistake, it's important not to shame them, but support them. I always do my best not to be critical, and encourage that in my singers too. I think if you watch The Sixteen on stage, you can see the support and forgiveness in their body language.

*Would you add humility to that list of qualities, too? You mentioned it earlier on, and I'm struck by the fact that those three singers – Padmore, Purves and Sampson – all seem to be humble, despite being musicians at the top of their game.*
Yes, they are; humble and incredibly musical.

*Tell me more about your singers. How much turnover has there been, over the years?*
Well, I realised gradually that I wanted people who were all thinking on the same wavelength, and could commit to the

group. When I look back through the 1990s to the present day, I realise I've become much more conscious of needing to have regular members. In the very early days, the group was often quite disparate, because I had to vary the top line a lot to accommodate the repertoire of Handel and Bach we were doing with Ton Koopman. The singer who's been with us longest is Sally Dunkley. She's now stepped down as a regular member, but often comes in and sings with us still, and is very involved in Genesis Sixteen. She is a legend among the other sopranos, and a great person to have around.

I'm very loyal to my singers. Only on a handful of occasions have I had to suggest it's not working and ask someone to leave – but that's very rare. By and large, either people have wanted to go on to a solo career – all of them successful – or they have wanted to stop singing altogether.

*How much of an impact did the recording industry have on the sound of the group?*

It had a huge impact. I would say that the recording industry shaped the sound of the group, and the industry's demise has also been the reason for all sorts of developments in the group's history. When we were making those early recordings, we had to make sure the choir had a wonderful sound, totally in style with the music we were singing. I have always spent time making sure the balance of the group is right. I go for opposites: putting a warmer voice next to a crystal-clear one. I take voices and let them be as they are. That's always been the nature of the group. We were able to focus on the music we loved because of artist-led labels like Hyperion. Ted Perry let us record several albums of Fayrfax, Sheppard and Taverner – he just loved Tudor music.

*And does the environment of the recording studio invite a different sound to a concert hall?*
It's mainly practical, in that I always get the whole choir in to listen back when we're doing a recording session, so they can hear first-hand what it sounds like. If younger singers aren't facially expressive, I tell them to sing into a mirror; listening back in recording sessions is the same thing. You can say something to the singers about words – I can't hear them, they don't make sense, there are consonants flying out that aren't important – and they don't believe me until they come in and listen to the playback. When they hear it, they realise whatever it is I've been going on about. They're intelligent singers and they can hear that they stick out like a sore thumb.

Those early Sheppard discs were done in only three sessions each. I've always wanted more of a feeling of a performance in recordings. When I listen back, I'm sometimes just considering whether I can cope with a rough edge or not – because I want that live edge. The recording industry made us all perfectionists, and ran the risk of making us into machines. I remember one producer we worked with wanted everything seamless, and the whole sound was wrong. The group just didn't sound like The Sixteen – it sounded like a manufactured sound. I hear that in a lot of groups recording now: they enhance the sound or edit it so much that it's absolutely perfect, but what they invariably lose is the soul of the music. I would hope when people listen to our recordings that they hear the soul of the music. I like doing longer

takes. If we're recording a whole motet lasting fifteen minutes, for example, I'll do it through once in its entirety, so
the producer knows the framework, and then we'll do it in
shorter sections and tweak things.

Back in the early days of recordings, we recorded almost
too much – we didn't always get the chance to perform the
same repertoire in concert. We were going from one thing to
the next too quickly. In one year, we recorded discs of Poulenc, Byrd, Handel and Tallis. It was exciting, but I wouldn't
do it again. That continued for the best part of ten years.
Then the CD industry completely imploded, and we were
forced to change our model. That's when we started doing
the Choral Pilgrimage. We looked to the model of the pop
world: the Rolling Stones do an album, and then they tour
it. We were very much a recording group to start with, it was
great to have all that work during the industry's heyday, but
what the choir is best at doing is performing live, and it's
what we love most.

*We'll come back to the recording industry and the group's cur-
rent working model in our next conversation. But for now, let's
return to The Sixteen's sound. Is it very different depending on
what repertoire you're performing?*
I would hope so. Even within the Renaissance repertoire, the
difference between Sheppard and Victoria has to come
across. Of course, a lot of it is down to the interpretation of
the work rather than the sound in particular – especially
when it comes to Victoria or Francisco Guerrero. Somehow,
music by those Iberian composers leaves more space for
interpretation. It has something to do with the passion of it,

I think. With Palestrina, I'm more concerned with breath than I am with interpretation. The group has to breathe together, so the music can have its ebb and flow. The 'Gloria' of *Missa Papae Marcelli*, for example, has to be conducted so it doesn't sound like it's chopped into segments – and to do that, you need breath. Breaths have to be part of the music to make sense of it; you can pull up into a rest, and let the music evolve after it, but the ebb and flow have to be there, and so do the light and shade.

The other really important thing is how you cadence. That's not about the penultimate note of a phrase, just to be clear. In the early days I used to linger on the penultimate note and think that was a good cadence. But I remember listening to the viol consort Fretwork, and thinking their cadences were just amazing, because they could be felt two or more bars before they happened. They weren't clinical or regimented, and they appeared as a logical conclusion of what had come before. I ask my singers to listen out for the line that is the driving force of the cadence. For example, I might draw their attention to a tenor line that dictates the cadence three bars later. Every cadence in the music will be different, each one a gesture. The most difficult thing is feeling that ebb and flow, and allowing the music to have a natural progression. And of course it always has to do with word stress and syntax, which is why I insist on my singers understanding the Latin they're singing. I don't do what Bernard Rose used to do, which was to try and tidy up a cadence.

*Isn't that tidying-up partly practical, a shorthand, to deal with the time constraints of a daily service in an Anglican setting?*

Yes, you're absolutely right – but within that limited rehearsal time you can still be particular. You can still have different parts coming off at slightly different times, according to their breath and phrase. Otherwise it sounds abrupt and regimented.

*And presumably it can also be laziness on the part of conductors. You strike me as the very opposite of a lazy conductor. Sally Dunkley mentioned that you always come very prepared to rehearsals. Is there an enormous amount of preparation for you, time spent poring over scores, or does it emerge more out of the rehearsal process?*

We have a limited amount of rehearsal, so I have to know what I'm doing. There are some people who go straight to rehearsal and hear the music as sung by the singers, and formulate things from there. If you're doing an opera, you can't come with too many fixed ideas beforehand because the production and cast have such a big impact on how it sounds. But with The Sixteen it's different. I get a score out, and the first thing I do is look at the words. I make sure I know what every single word means, and I see how the music relates to that. Because I've done a lot of Renaissance music, I'll look to see where there's a special, purple passage. By that, I mean a passage with perhaps some striking textural variety, a different number of voices, something harmonic that stands out. I'll mark that in my score. I don't make too many markings, but I'll note specific imitative entries, or if I think a certain part should be leading a particular passage. I talk about 'points' when I'm rehearsing – the new point is the new imitative phrase.

I come to our rehearsals prepared, and go through the markings with everyone before we sing a piece through for the first time. I give them dynamics, as a guide, and talk about the rhythmic feel of the music. The *tactus* is the heart-beat of the music: faster if joyous, slower if more penitential. I use my acquired knowledge of Renaissance music to notice certain points in the text where the composer would likely make the music still, a special moment of reverence. Then we rehearse the piece, and if there are certain things I've marked that aren't working, I'll change them. I try to get the singers to feel the ends of phrases, clearing words or con-sonants in a way that feels right. We might mark in breaths, and often a singer will ask for more time to breathe in a particular place, and we'll try it a few times to see if we can accommodate it. I try not to straitjacket the music, and I'm always prepared to make a change if something doesn't feel or sound right.

The way I work on or conduct a piece of music will partly depend on who it's by, or what it is. Having done sixteenth-century music for so many years, a lot of this comes as second nature. We are now up to Volume 7 of our Palestrina recordings, and I constantly feel a pressure to come up with something new or different in my interpret-ation, and then I remember that sometimes, I can just let the music speak for itself. Palestrina is so brilliant, such a craftsman. With Victoria, as I've said, I'm more interested in putting my interpretive stamp on it. Sheppard's writing, similarly, is easier to 'interpret' than Byrd. In Byrd, there is often so much going on, you need to get behind the phrase and articulate things in a particular way for it to work.

I find ways to coax light, shade and transparency from the music, and using dynamics subtly is one way to do that. If you mark in a block *crescendo* – where everyone in the choir gets louder at the same time, together – it can sound too much like a choral society. I might, for example, ask the sopranos to put a phrase in brackets, so that it doesn't become too prominent, something that is really more filigree or ornamental. And I always remember back to David Wulstan talking about the architecture of phrases, and the idea of a phrase having a peak note. But it's no good just bashing out the top note if you then ignore the descending phrase that follows.

Relaxation is also so important. Conductors can look so tense, but if the sopranos are hitting a top note, I have to use a gentle gesture. If you shake your hands at them, with tension, it will make things much harder for them.

*It sounds, then, as though your job as conductor is more as a facilitator, making things easier for your singers. How do you balance that with your desire to put your own stamp on the music?*
The interpretation comes first and foremost, I suppose, and not everybody in the group may like what I do, but they have enough faith in me to know it will work as an entity. When I feel singers or sections of the group making a phrase their own, it's just wonderful and special. I am a facilitator in that way. I also feel I have total control, but that's because the singers always have their eyes on me. They know I could do something completely different to rehearsal, and spontaneous.

Spontaneity is very important to me, as we move from the rehearsal studio to the concert hall or cathedral. In over 250 performances of Handel's *Messiah*, I don't think I've ever done the same thing twice. I think the Choral Pilgrimage has survived because we do around thirty *different* performances of the same programme. We visit so many different buildings, and each one is unique. Take Durham Cathedral, for example. It's the most beautiful building, but it's very hard for the choir to sing in, because they can't hear each other. I remember one year we did a Josquin programme in Durham, and there was a moment of very difficult ensemble singing to keep in synch. The singers had to watch me and trust me so that it stayed together. No matter how good you are as a singer, a performer, a musician, different buildings or venues can be hard on you, particularly if the acoustic is dry and nothing comes back to you. I often ask the singers to exaggerate shapes in the music if the building isn't helping us. That involves trust, both ways.

*Let's stop there, because you've brought us beautifully to the starting-point of our next conversation, about the Choral Pilgrimage, and the life of the group today.*

# FOUR

# The Life of The Sixteen

As I set off for Kent for what turns out to be the last time (our subsequent conversations take place at my home in London), I listen on headphones to *Vadam et circuibo*, an anthem by Victoria. The text, from the Song of Songs, describes searching through the city's streets. I am so absorbed in Victoria's polyphony that I barely notice London through the train windows, and the sidings carpeted with snow.

Harry has set me this piece to listen to as a starting point for our conversation about the main activities that underpin the work of The Sixteen today: the Choral Pilgrimage, and the group's own record label, CORO.

Victoria crops up in several of the Choral Pilgrimage programmes; two of them, from 2006 and 2011, are dedicated exclusively to the work of the Spanish Renaissance master. *Vadam et circuibo* was part of *The Call of the Beloved*, and appears on yet another Choral Pilgrimage disc called *The Flowering of Genius*. It is exquisitely sung by an ensemble which includes singers who have gone to successful solo careers, such as Carolyn Sampson and James Gilchrist.

When I arrive in Harry's conservatory, a stack of A4 programme booklets is waiting for me on the coffee table. He has assembled every Choral Pilgrimage programme to date for me to look through, and they make impressive reading. The Pilgrimages have covered a vast range of repertoire, from Josquin to James MacMillan, and each one is skilfully crafted, successful as both a recording and a concert experience. Each booklet contains thoroughly researched articles – though never so scholarly as to alienate the reader – and some of the programmes are flexible enough to be tailored to the individual cathedrals in which The Sixteen performed that year.

We begin by talking about Victoria.

❧

*You've recorded a huge amount of Victoria's music over the years, and he's clearly a favourite of yours. Why is that?*
Predominantly because of his understanding of text. He was a priest, a mystic, an organist and a composer, absolutely devoted to the church, and his insight into the liturgy was exceptional. And somehow, even though he spent most of his life in Rome, he maintained his Iberian roots.

*How is his music Iberian in style?*
There is something slightly different about the music of the Spanish composers of the Renaissance. The likes of Victoria, Guerrero, Cristóbal de Morales and Alonso Lobo all have something in common. What's unique about their music is mirrored in architecture: Spanish cathedrals are dripping with gold, and you feel that these composers have their heart more in the music than their Italian contemporaries. It's hard to explain, but it comes across in the music. Victoria's Requiem, for example, stands out above all other Requiems. His penitential music is particularly heart-rending.

*So it has more to do with emotion, something intangible, rather than the musical construction? I ask because Victoria's music can be as simple as Tallis. I'm thinking, for example, of the 'Kyrie' of the Requiem, which is simple, relatively homophonic music.*

Exactly. The same is true of *O vos omnes*, a motet from the *Tenebrae* music. It is simply gorgeous. But then you get to something like *Vadam* . . .

*Which I listened to . . .*

It's one of my favourite Renaissance pieces. Victoria had spent time in Italy, under the influence of Palestrina, that god of music, but by the time he wrote this piece, he had moved back to spend his last years in Madrid. It begins with 'Vadam et circuibo': I will rise now, and go about the city – and it has these wandering phrases, weaving and winding round like the writer through the streets. Then it opens out and becomes so sensual and full of passion on the words 'dilectum meum', meaning 'my beloved'. At the end of the first section, in which the writer is looking for that beloved, Victoria uses repeated phrases, piling on the emotion. There's one amazing false relation in there too.

*I noticed that immediately when listening, and I wondered if it was one you had added, or was there in the edition you use.*

No, it's not one of my additions, and I'm sure Victoria did it on purpose – it's absolutely not in the Palestrina rulebook of polyphony. It may also be a clever pun, because immediately afterwards, the text is 'Talis est delectus meus', meaning 'this is my beloved'. But perhaps Victoria was picking up on the similarity to the name of Tallis, who relished his false relations.

*Is it likely that Victoria would have known Tallis's music?*
Yes. Well, Tallis lived for a long time, so they overlap. And Victoria's music would have been sung when Philip II of Spain came over to England to marry Queen Mary I.

*The recording I was listening to appears on the disc* The Flowering of Genius, *a programme that focuses on that moment of Catholic possibility in English history, with English composers like Tallis set against their Catholic contemporaries in Spain, such as Victoria and Guerrero.*
That whole sequence of Philip coming to England is fascinating. The musicologist John Milsom now has different theories about Tallis's 'Puer natus est' Mass, and why it was written, but it was long thought to have been for the occasion of Philip's visit and marriage to Mary, Queen of England. It is interesting that the tessitura of the voices it's written for is much more akin to the Spanish choir that Philip would have had in his service. Philip's Capilla Real joined forces with the choir of St Paul's Cathedral to sing Mass on Christmas Day. The Spanish choir wouldn't have used the higher voices of the English choirs, and therefore sounded more sonorous in the middle textures. Tallis, ever the pragmatist, wrote accordingly.

*That richness does seem to stand out in the Spanish music on the disc. As well as the emotional depth, there is a roundness to the sound that Victoria's music creates.*

The thing with Victoria is that he was also a singer. There's no doubt he knows the voice and writes for it well. The singers always comment on how comfortable the vocal lines are to sing. The architecture of the phrases suit the tessitura of each voice so well, and his word-painting is so extraordinarily beautiful you can't help but revel in it and enjoy it. Even in the starker pieces like the Requiem, which is much more homophonic, there are moments of repose. He uses silence very effectively.

He gets closest to letting his hair down in his settings of the Song of Songs. But he clearly never wanted to write madrigals, like Palestrina or Lassus did – he simply wanted to devote himself to the church, and wrote wonderful music for it.

*I notice that you seem particularly drawn to Catholic composers – Victoria, Tallis, Byrd, and even Poulenc. Why is that, given that you grew up in the Anglican Church?*

My wife Lonnie is a Catholic. When we met, her father was the director of music at Birmingham Oratory. He'd been a boy chorister under the direction of the organist H. B. Collins. Lonnie's father had a very Catholic way of doing things, very similar to George Malcolm at Westminster Cathedral – a lot of freedom, and you could say over-characterisation, and very 'high church'. I remember going to my first Mass at Birmingham Oratory, and I didn't warm to it particularly – the priests, mumbling away at the distant altar, felt completely out of touch with the congregation. But I did very much enjoy the music in the space. I found there was a sort of freedom to it. It was a strong contrast to the Anglican formality I had encountered in Canterbury, Magdalen and Westminster Abbey. In the Anglican Church, the pageantry is formalised. Everyone processes and turns together, says the Creed in unison; whereas the Catholics seemed to wander in and out of Mass when they wanted to, and that sense of freedom resonated for me with the music.

In England, we suffered a violent Reformation, and it's interesting to see how the composers of the day reacted to that. Tallis went with the flow, living through several reigns of kings and queens. Queen Elizabeth I clearly had a soft spot for Catholicism, although she wasn't at liberty to say so publicly; but she allowed Tallis and Byrd to write the *Cantiones sacrae* [three sets of publications of sacred music to Latin texts, published between 1575 and 1591] on the condition that there was no mention of the Virgin Mary. Byrd was always a Catholic, and unlike Tallis never wanted to make concessions to Protestantism, but as a result lived his whole life in fear.

*Having sung music by both Byrd and Victoria, I sense a connection between them – am I right? Perhaps it's because they're Catholic, but it seems there's something else too, about how the music sits on the voice. Their phrases seem to unfold in such a way that the voice can expand – it's not restricted.*

Yes, that's right. Byrd's music is easy to sing in one sense, but it is also staggering in its virtuosity. It can be tricky to find a way around the various motifs of his more complex pieces. We often perform one of Byrd's eight-part motets, *Ad Dominum*. It's an early work with a thick texture, and it has a monolithic feel to it. You have to rely on Byrd to carry you through, and pay attention to the imitation of parts. There were so many composers in England at that time writing in a much older style, but Byrd was constantly pushing boundaries and looking forward.

What you say about the music fitting the voice applies to Tallis too. He really knew about singing. Apart from his big antiphons like *Gaude gloriosa*, most of his music is based on plainsong. Understanding the voice, understanding text, is part and parcel of music of that period. The cathedrals in which these composers worked were built with music in mind; and the composers were writing music with these buildings in mind.

*You encounter many of these cathedrals each year on your Choral Pilgrimage. How did the project come about?*
It began in 2000, for the millennium, and it was a simple idea. Throughout the 1990s, we would rehearse a programme, give a concert, make a recording, and then put the piece away and move on to the next project. We started thinking about whether that model worked, and how to continue. At the same time, we wanted to do something special for the millennium. We had toyed with the idea of commissioning a new work, but it hadn't worked out. At the time, Anthony Smith [President of Magdalen College, Oxford, 1988–2005] was the chair of our development board, and he suggested that instead of doing more concerts in London, we should be doing a tour of England's finest cathedrals. At first, I had financial concerns about putting on concerts outside London; musicians are so often focused on the capital. The usual model is that you save up money to perform a series of

concerts in St John's Smith Square, and then other engagements spring from it. But when we began to think about it, we realised what a lovely thing it would be to go further afield. We were fighting hard to get an audience of 250 at St John's as it was, and it was costing us a fortune. So we gave this new idea a chance.

Over roughly eight months, we performed in twelve cathedrals. Our strap-line was: 'Inspiring music in England's finest cathedrals'. The programme booklet contained a foreword by Simon Jenkins, the journalist and author of several books about England's cathedrals and churches. We began in York, and travelled on to Durham, Gloucester, Chester, Winchester, Oxford, Salisbury, Liverpool, Lincoln, Birmingham, Wells and ended up in Canterbury.

*Had you been to all those buildings yourself, before you set off?*
No. I didn't know Chester, Liverpool or Wells. Wells Cathedral was an eye-opener; it's a phenomenal building. The idea was to bring pre-Reformation music back to these buildings, many of which the music was designed for. In each cathedral, we did a slightly different programme, relevant to that building; for example, we did music by Robert White in Chester, and Richard Hygons – an Eton Choirbook composer – in Wells. We asked the Pevsner Architectural Guides if we could include something in the programme about each building, and they agreed. In both York and Canterbury we performed Tallis's *Spem in alium*, that great forty-part motet. Naturally, we needed extra singers, so in York we were joined by the choir of York Minster, and in Canterbury we splashed out on an enlarged group of The Sixteen.

There was a great deal of national coverage in the press. Of course, these cathedrals put on concerts already, and had groups touring to them, but no other single group was doing such a large tour to so many. On paper, it looked like financial madness. Most of these cathedrals had no infrastructure for ticket sales, so we had to get local box offices to help us, and we only had two or three people in our own office making it all happen. But somehow it worked. In York, over a thousand people turned up, and the nave of the cathedral was packed. Not all of them were quite that full, but over the years we have built good relationships with the cathedrals and local audiences. Now, we give about thirty concerts in each Pilgrimage.

*Does it actually feel like a pilgrimage?*
Yes, it does. Of course, we're not walking, but it does in the sense that we meet people along the way, they thank us for coming, we thank them for hosting us, and it feels like a real journey. It's socially rewarding within the group too. From our first Pilgrimage, it has been a great pleasure for the whole choir to sing this music in these buildings. We had been spending our time up until then singing it in concert halls, but suddenly encountering a different acoustic was a revelation.

*What difference does the acoustic of a cathedral make, as opposed to a concert hall?*
Every building is different. Some are more difficult to sing in for the choir, but some are just glorious. Their favourite place is Tewkesbury Abbey. York also takes some beating.

After the choir's first concert in York, they all said what a privilege it was to perform this music to the audience, but also to feel the music resounding around the stonework and firing off the building. Some buildings may sound better than others, but they are all special.

*Is there something particular about the acoustics of English cathedrals that means you end up singing or making music in a different way?*

The real difference is in the silences – they are magical, the way a final chord resounds in the space. Roger Bray [Magdalen graduate and musicologist] wrote an article in one of our programmes explaining that all these cathedrals, particularly the Norman ones, were built on the same basic ratio. A lot of the cathedrals have been tampered with over the years, and very often it's in those alterations that the sound also changes. When you sing in Chichester or Peterborough the sound seems to be constant all the way down the nave; in others, the chords might distort as you move around, or the sound suddenly lose its bloom three-quarters of the way down the nave. The beauty of it is finding a way to work each space. Because we do thirty concerts each time, we know the programme well, and often we have only half an hour of rehearsal, and we spend most of that figuring out how to use the space well. We always perform in the naves, singing down the mass of the building. What keeps those concerts alive is actually not doing too much rehearsal on the day; instead, we can hear things spontaneously in the concert and adapt.

I am so pleased with how the Pilgrimage has taken off and

become the framework of The Sixteen's concert season. And the other aspect of it is the CD we record, which makes a lot of financial sense, because people want to take away a physical copy of what they've just heard.

*Let's talk about the actual programmes you put together – again, they are such a distinctive aspect of The Sixteen. How do you begin to put a Choral Pilgrimage programme together?*
I begin with a blank piece of paper, and then choose a single piece or a vague theme. In 2010, for example, for the Pilgrimage's tenth anniversary, I wanted to perform Sheppard's *Media vita*, a large-scale work, and I constructed the programme around it. I have a number of people I ask for advice and suggestions of what pieces would be interesting to start with. Martyn Imrie is my guru for Spanish and Italian Renaissance repertoire. He lives on a Scottish island, and though we've corresponded a lot, we've actually never met. I will ask Sally Dunkley for advice about the Tudor repertoire, and John Milsom is also a great source of inspiration.

So, using the first piece as a starting-point, I will come up with an idea to draw the programme together. Sometimes, I choose that piece based on a financial imperative. For example, our 2013 Choral Pilgrimage programme, *Queen of Heaven*, began with me saying I wanted to do the Allegri *Miserere*, to ensure we got a good audience. Then, I added James Mac-Millan's *Miserere* to the programme. And rather than do the Allegri straight, I put together what I described as an 'evolution version' of it, showing how it has changed over the years. The work is shrouded in mystery, and the Vatican library has, until recently, been rather chaotic. The only version of Allegri's

*Miserere* that survives is from a few years after Allegri's death, and that was followed by other, later versions. So Ben Byram-Wigfield, who had done a lot of research on the various sources, helped me put together a score that went through the ages and ended up with what we most commonly hear today. The piece is known for its top C, but that in itself is totally wrong, a scribal error. Halfway through the solo quartet, the second soprano leaps up a fourth; but it's a mistake. Remember, in the Sistine Chapel they had castrati on the first row, who certainly wouldn't have been able to sing those top Cs. Now, it may be wrong, but it's also beautiful. It's rather like a painting by Botticelli which turns out to be falsely attributed; it doesn't take away from the beauty of the painting. So, I had two pieces, the Allegri version and MacMillan's *Miserere*, which framed the programme, and then I worked other pieces and themes into it.

It has become more difficult as the years go on to find original ideas. Some ideas will come from a commission or an invitation. I remember being asked by a festival in the Concertgebouw Brugge in Belgium to put together a programme with the theme of the Alps. I thought of composers who had crossed the Alps for employment: Josquin, Lassus and Antoine Brumel. This became *The Earth Resounds*, our 2012 Choral Pilgrimage, one of our most popular programmes to date. My starting piece was the so-called 'Earthquake' Mass by Brumel, which is based on the plainsong *Et ecce terrae motus*: 'and behold, the earth moved'. Because it's large and I needed extra singers for it, I thought it was a good excuse to do a magnificent double-choir work by Lassus, *Aurora lucis rutilat*. I then brought in music by Josquin which

Lassus based his *Magnificat* on. In Renaissance music, there is a lot to latch on to as a programmer, with parody masses, in which composers paid homage to other composers.

In another programme I knew I wanted to concentrate on Byrd, but was struggling to find a composer to go well with him – and then I suddenly thought of Arvo Pärt, because his sound-world is so utterly different, with silences and chords dropping in. It makes a wonderful contrast to the monolithic and solid texture of Byrd's *Ad Dominum*.

*I'm struck by the breadth of your repertoire. Anyone in the classical music industry will tell you there's an enormous pressure to programme repertoire that audiences feel comfortable with. It's very difficult to sell contemporary music – there's a school of thought that says you need a Tchaikovsky symphony in the second half to make it palatable. Whereas with The Sixteen, you manage to fill a cathedral with an audience for Lassus and Brumel. Most people have never heard of Brumel, even music lovers. Your audiences can't be looking at the composers billed and coming because of them.*

No, I would say about half our audience have never heard of the composers we sing. But the Choral Pilgrimage has become such a large part of our existence that audiences trust us. If we think it's worth hearing, they trust that. There are several factors that went into building that trust and our reputation. Our association with Classic FM had a massive impact; we are the Voices of Classic FM. The agreement with them was simple: they advertised our concerts, and we put their branding on our print material. They would play a track from the album, and people would hear it and come to our concerts. *Sacred Music*, the BBC Four television series we made with Simon Russell Beale from 2009 onwards, had even more of an impact in helping to build our audience. And word spreads. A lot of the Choral Pilgrimage concerts are our own promotions, but several festivals have also invited us to perform at them.

The Choral Pilgrimage also started at a time when people were still buying CDs. We had done so many recordings by that point that we were often played on BBC Radio 3 and Classic FM. In the 1990s and early 2000s, early and Renaissance polyphony went from being music that the cognoscenti enjoyed, to having a far wider popular appeal. People found that it had a meditative quality, that it could calm you down after a long car journey or a bad day at work. I would speak to people in our audiences and they would say they had been taken to another world listening to our music. Most of those audience members wouldn't go to church, but loved to hear the music in these splendid buildings.

I think people also love to hear The Sixteen perform because even singing in the big nave of a cathedral, they have the feeling that we are alive and performing directly to them. They can see our eyes and faces communicating the music. I press that point on my singers all the time. When you go to the theatre you don't just hear words, you see the actor's face. With singers, it's the same. If their faces lack expression, I don't see the point in a concert.

When I started working with the Handel and Haydn Society in Boston, I remember a newspaper critic interviewed me about audiences. I said I wanted to get the musicians out of their seats, reacting to baroque music more physically, because the music is so based on dance. The critic replied that it would be off-putting to see an orchestral musician who wasn't sitting still in their seat. So I asked: in that case, why not just stay home and listen to the CD? Of course, as I've said before, I want our recordings to have the rough edges of a live performance too. People need to hear humanity, humility and rough edges, because we are human and fragile, and we make mistakes. My singers are vibrant personalities with great voices, and their characters have to come across in concert and on disc.

*Are the audiences for the Choral Pilgrimage concerts very different from those who come and hear you in concert halls? Cathedrals, although imposing, are public buildings. Do you think that local communities feel a sense of ownership of their cathedrals that they don't of their concert halls?*

Yes. And it isn't just local communities; there are plenty of people who come and hear us in several different venues on one or more Choral Pilgrimage tours. The series has become a very social event. As with a lot of classical music, the age range tends to be on the older side, but when we visit university cities like York, Durham, Birmingham and Liverpool, it's very noticeable – we get a lot of university students coming to hear us. That is very comforting, to know that there are young people still inspired by this music. I'm fascinated by how many people apply for our Genesis Sixteen programme each year – which we will discuss another day. But the interest there is just staggering.

But you mention the difference between a church and a concert hall, and of course a church is a sacred venue. That can put people off. We are singing sacred music in those spaces, and the images on our concert brochures tend to be sacred images, so we have to be careful about that.

The other thing you mentioned is about the repertoire. Although our audiences trust us, they do come with preconceptions. There have been the inevitable comments when we've programmed Poulenc or MacMillan; people say they are nervous about that unknown repertoire. But once they come to the concert, they adore it. Poulenc's *Un soir de neige*, for example, won them over completely. James MacMillan's *Miserere* was gut-churning, and everyone who came walked out of the concert talking about it, and not about the more famous Allegri.

The same goes for a programme we did in 2004. It was all Portuguese music, called *A Golden Age*. We didn't announce any of the repertoire on the front of the programme. Back in the early 1990s, the Gulbenkian Foundation had sent me a lot of editions of Portuguese music, so we put together a programme of better-known composers like Domenico Scarlatti – who had been employed by the royal court in Lisbon – and lesser-known ones such as Jõao Lourenço Rebelo and Diogo Dias Melgás. The piece that really had people talking was the *Lamentations* by Melgás. It's incredibly static music, very simple, but with printed individual continuo lines for harp, lute and organ. It sounded amazingly effective in those buildings, and our audiences loved it.

There's one final thing about putting together programmes I should mention, and that's their length. I tend to have a larger work in each half which acts as a linchpin. But I make sure that neither half is too long. Thirty-five minutes of music in each half of the concert is enough; we start at half past seven, and finish at ten past nine, and I think that is the perfect length. Some of these cathedrals are pretty chilly in the winter months, and audiences also want to go out for a meal afterwards. So a lot of thought goes into making the Choral Pilgrimage a lovely evening out.

The same applies to the concerts we do outside the Choral Pilgrimage. We have our Christmas tour, which visits around eight venues, and we also do a tour with the choir and orchestra early in each year. All in all, we think around 40,000 people in the UK hear us live every year.

*Who are you making music for? Is the intention to reach as many people as possible?*

Oh yes, absolutely. As many people, and often in places that don't have much music provision, such as Carlisle Cathedral, Lancaster Priory, Sheffield Cathedral, or Holy Trinity Church in Hull, which we visited when they had just started the repairs for the forthcoming City of Culture celebrations. The city of Hull is full of beautiful facades, and used to be a great port. The communities in all these places who came to our concerts were really wonderful. That is the most impressive and also humbling thing about the experience of the Choral Pilgrimage, getting the chance to meet people who come to our concerts and chat with them in the pub afterwards.

*What strikes me about your ambition for the group, in terms of audiences, is that it is the opposite of elitist – to use a rather loaded word. You come from what could be described as an elite background – public school, studying music at Oxford – and yet your approach to making music seems to be very broad and democratic. You speak about what resonates with you emotionally, rather than critical opinion or indeed academic value. The music world can be a bubble, but you seem to want to break beyond that. Why is that, I wonder?*

I'm not sure. I think it's because I make music because I love it. The day this music becomes a chore to me will be the day I stop doing it. I'm not very good on my own. I'm a very sociable person and always have been, and part of a choir's existence is the experience of being in a family. The ultimate goal for our performers is to serve their audiences in the best possible way. Nobody goes into music or the arts to become a millionaire. I started with nothing, and I'm very lucky that everything has built in the way it has, and I can live in a nice house. But I'm not one of those big maestro types. Music isn't about that for me – it's about bringing the best out in my performers, and inspiring the audiences behind me. It's as simple as that.

And while I do know a lot about this music, because I've done so much of it, I'm not an academic. My parents never went to concerts, I wasn't brought up that way, and it's not in my psyche. I don't have an encyclopaedic knowledge of orchestral music as so many conductors do. I played orchestral music at school, but everything I do with an orchestra is new to me, every opera I conduct is new to me, and I try to do as much choral music as I can that's new to me too. So I try to come with a totally fresh approach, uninfluenced by recordings – if indeed there are recordings of the rare repertoire we perform – and I feel very lucky that somehow it has worked.

*If I look at the way you've constructed The Sixteen's business –
being the Voices of Classic FM, the exposure you got through the
BBC Four series* Sacred Music, *and the way the Choral Pilgrimage has gathered audiences like moss to a stone over the
years – I might be led to think that you set out specifically to
popularise Renaissance repertoire, to develop a more democratic
profile for it with a broader reach. Was that your explicit aim,
back in the late 1990s?*

Not explicit, no. In fact, the success of The Sixteen since the
Choral Pilgrimage started has happened slightly by accident.
I have always had good people working behind the scenes,
who, at crucial points, have taken an idea of mine and run
with it. In 1994, for example, we were bubbling away, working out of an agency, and suddenly realised we had lost
£40,000 on an American tour and a run of four *Messiah*s at
St John's Smith Square. The situation was dire. So from one
day to the next, we moved out of Magenta Music, moved
into the front room of a friend's house in north London,
and by chance managed to get Sarah Tenant-Flowers to
come and work for us. Between her and Peter Burrows, they
turned us from £100,000 in the red to being in the black, in
the space of eighteen months. We wrote a frank letter to the
Foundation for Sport and the Arts, saying we had messed
up, and that we were putting together a business plan to get
ourselves back on track; we got an unconditional donation
from them. I had to remortgage my house, and Lonnie,
despite the incredible risk, stood behind me at all times.
And we have always had a supportive board, who have
helped to keep our mission clear.

*So what is the mission of The Sixteen?*
It is to bring the music of our past to a greater audience. We're not about educating, we're about inspiring listeners and students to come into this magical world of music. And it's also to prevent this legacy of music from being lost. To be honest, although collegiate and cathedral choirs up and down the country do a wonderful job, if not for groups like us many of the larger works would get lost. No Dean and Chapter wants to sit through a fifteen-minute antiphon on a wet Thursday afternoon or at Sunday Evensong when there's also a long sermon.

The Choral Pilgrimage is something I worked really hard on, but we were also lucky that it was a success, and we rolled with it. We occasionally overstretch ourselves, but only where we know we can. We run a very tight organisation. I've always maintained that every five or ten years you have to re-evaluate what you do, and perhaps reinvent yourself.

Everybody who's worked with The Sixteen over the years has realised that we are normal people who love what we do.

*The founding of CORO was something I wanted to talk briefly about too . . . When did you found it, and why?*
It began in 2001. We had already been recording for many years, and for the best part of a decade I had been able to record whatever I wanted. In 1998, our record company Collins folded. We already had discs on Hyperion, Chandos and Virgin, but on Collins alone we had a catalogue of thirty-two recordings, all of them music I had wanted to do, such as the Eton Choirbook series, and the Victoria series, Handel oratorios *Esther* and *Samson*, music by Britten and Messiaen,

and Poulenc as well. All of it was music I had put my heart and soul into.

When Collins folded, and we saw bits of their catalogue being sold off to other labels, we felt so sad. We worried that the catalogue would get dispersed, or lost, and that we would never get them back. In putting together our first Choral Pilgrimage disc, Phil Hobbs of Linn Records had licensed all the tracks for us, and it was such a success that we thought we would try to buy back the Collins catalogue. We went for a meeting with Collins, showed them what we had just produced for our Choral Pilgrimage, compared it to one of the budget labels they were selling their catalogue to, and tried to persuade them. They pointed out that they had spent nearly £1 million on us over the years, and said it would cost the best part of £100,000 to buy back the catalogue, which of course we didn't have. So we put forward a plan to set up our own company and re-release six or so of the CDs each year, over four or five years. We laid out a repayment plan, and after a day of lawyers thrashing out a deal, they agreed. From the sales we made from that back catalogue, we made enough income to record a new disc each year. Everybody told us we were mad, forming a record company when the classical CD industry was in major decline – but it worked.

So far, it has continued well, with the money we make from CORO being ploughed back into The Sixteen and new recordings. But now, we have to find extra ways of raising money for it. CORO has a stand at every Choral Pilgrimage concert. The two are intertwined. As I think I mentioned before, we're like the Rolling Stones: we record the album, and then we take it on tour.

*You know the recording industry from the inside, having been a part of it since the beginnings of The Sixteen. In that time, it has gone through many changes. What is your take on the health of the industry now?*

The industry is not doing well. In fact, its history has been very short. The CD first came out in 1982, devised by Sony and Philips. Funnily enough, most people think that Abba were the first group to release a CD. Theirs was the first pressed, but the first commercially released CD was a disc of the pianist Claudio Arrau performing Chopin waltzes. Even so, it took the classical industry a while to cotton on. Dire Straits had already sold millions by the time the classical industry started recording CDs.

It went hand in hand with the early-music movement. People had already started editing and researching early music, but when the CD companies came along, they injected a huge amount of money and energy into that part of the industry, resulting in great projects by people like Paul McCreesh and Andrew Parrott. The CD invigorated classical music. But its heyday was short-lived, from around the mid-1980s to the mid-1990s. In that time, CD companies went berserk, throwing money at recordings while we performers lapped it up. The sad thing is that many of the groups who geared themselves entirely towards recordings ended up collapsing when the money ran out.

The Sixteen nearly suffered the same fate. In the 1990s, we relied too heavily on CDs, because we thought that the more we recorded, the more concerts we would generate. We were wrong, and nowadays we realise it's the other way round: our CDs need to be a reflection of our concert life.

*That is very much the model which CORO was founded on, taken, as you've said, from the pop world rather than the classical. You record an album and then you take it on tour, and sell the CDs at your concerts. Is that model still working for you?*

At CORO, we pride ourselves on how many CDs we sell at Choral Pilgrimage concerts, which make up a lot of our overall sales. Even so, we have noticed a significant drop over the last couple of years in how many CDs we have sold at concerts. That is partly dependent on ticket sales – if our ticket sales are lower one year, our CD sales will be too. And we take a real risk with audience numbers when we programme unknown repertoire. As we discussed when talking about the Choral Pilgrimage, I make a point of being brave with the repertoire we perform. I won't just roll out old favourites like the Allegri *Miserere* year after year just to sell more tickets. I think audiences are even scared of composers like Poulenc and Britten. It's the same problem arts organisations everywhere are grappling with: how to draw in audiences for unfamiliar repertoire.

*What you've just described – that you sell most of your CDs at concerts rather than online – is unusual, isn't it?*

Yes, it is unusual. Recently, though, while we have noticed a drop in CD sales, we have seen a rise in digital sales. There will always be people out there who want to own a physical CD, but the younger listeners are different. Most importantly, the Choral Pilgrimage has had a big impact on our public image, and people's awareness of it has increased their interest in our recordings. We invested heavily in digital downloads, which we now offer through our website. The leaders in that field are

Hyperion – their website is terrific, and they made a huge investment in it. The other interesting trend we have noticed is that during most of the year, people will buy single tracks rather than a whole album, even just a single movement of a Mass; but at certain times of year, most of all Christmas, they will buy a whole album. So in response, we often record a special Christmas album, as we are doing this year.

*Is it ever going to stop being worth you recording CDs?*
I hope not. In the short term, I don't see us stopping, nor in the long term, in fact. If you want to be recognised world-wide as a performing group, you have to have recorded material for radio stations to play, and I think we are getting more savvy about that in the UK than ever before. As musicians, we need to realise that there's no money to be had in making CDs anymore, but you need to have them.

*So recordings are effectively part of a marketing strategy?*
Yes, in a way. And we need to continue to persuade our donors why CDs are worth recording. At the moment, we are very lucky at The Sixteen to have a board who understand that recordings are worthwhile, both for our public profile, and because we are making recordings of interesting music for posterity.

*Despite CORO's success, the industry as a whole is in decline. Given that its heyday was such a big part of The Sixteen's early success, does that decline make you sad?*
In one respect I don't feel sad about it at all, because the way the industry worked turned us musicians into recording

machines. We ran the risk of recording too much, and not performing enough for live audiences. At the same time, all the money that was being ploughed into the recording industry meant that we were able to afford the time it took to rehearse a lot of really obscure repertoire, which these days it's harder to justify as an expense. Nowadays, there just isn't the equivalent funding to allow lengthy rehearsals of new material. That's why the Choral Pilgrimage is so rewarding, because we put a huge amount of effort into rehearsing one single programme, and then tour it, during which time we get to know the repertoire better than ever before. And if I'm putting together a special, one-off programme – for example, the concert you heard at Kings Place, *Book of Hours* – I will always include a large work that the group knows well already. We ended that concert with Anerio's *Magnificat*, which we had previously performed on a Choral Pilgrimage, and it was like meeting an old friend – the group just slotted back into singing it incredibly well.

*Before we finish, tell me briefly about* Sacred Music *on BBC Four, with Simon Russell Beale. How did it come about?*
The BBC producer Helen Mansfield asked to meet up with me one day to chat about a possible series. She had seen the success of the Choral Pilgrimage, the fact that people wanted to come to concerts of sacred music, and that we were making it popular. She had an idea for a series, and we discussed all sorts of aspects of what we could do for it – it was only to be four episodes, so we had to start with the birth of polyphony. It was so popular that the BBC commissioned a second series, as well as a number of one-off programmes.

The first episode was filmed in the church of Saint-Denis in Paris with just four singers. We filmed it in one day. The music, early French polyphony, was light years away from anything I'd ever performed before. But it was fascinating. I had to go back to school to learn about it all, really, and find out about how it was sung, and experiment. But because the show was a documentary rather than performance-related, we discussed a lot about who was going to be a presenter, and we landed on Simon Russell Beale. He'd been a chorister at St Paul's and a choral scholar at Cambridge, and then went to Guildhall as a singer before switching to acting. He was an inspired choice, and he loved it; it was a really successful format.

After that first episode, we made one about Byrd and Tallis, another on Luther and Bach, and also a whole episode on Palestrina. It was all filmed on location, with beautiful camerawork. I was also involved in trying to find locations. For Bach, we found the first Lutheran church in Aldgate built by the German community there, who were all sugar dealers. We went up to Waltham Abbey to do Tallis, and to Stondon Massey, Byrd's home in Essex, to sing the 'Agnus Dei' from his Mass in Four Parts round the table in the very room where they would have sung Mass as recusant Catholics.

But the first one in Saint-Denis was the most memorable. We were all taken aback. I imagine it was a bit like being there when Stravinsky's *The Rite of Spring* was first heard. To imagine what the congregation would have made of the first time they heard Léonin, all that droning and wailing; some of them must have thought it was brilliant and wacky, while others would have hated every minute. And then to hear the two-part music develop into the three- or four-part music of Pérotin was a revelation. We heard how the sound went back evenly through the space of Saint-Denis. That doesn't happen so much today in Notre-Dame, the cathedral where a lot of this music originated, because the building has been added to, which changes the acoustic.

Putting that programme together involved a lot of experimentation for us. It was interesting playing around with it all. All the comments sent in to the BBC afterwards said it didn't dumb down, nor did it go over people's heads.

*That's a perfect description of what I was trying to get at earlier, your non-elitist way of making music. You don't dumb down with The Sixteen, nor do you exclude people or make it feel like an elite art.*
I would hope that is true.

# FIVE

# Sir James MacMillan
# and Genesis Sixteen

The following day, a planned fifth conversation has to be postponed because of the snow. It has finally undone the rail network, and Otford trains are cancelled and delayed. Rather than risk my getting stranded, we agree to leave it another week, and meet instead in London.

The day before we convene again, in early March, an excited email arrives from Harry. He has just received the manuscript of the new commission from James MacMillan, *O Virgo prudentissima*. The group will be performing it in Eton Chapel and then taking it on the Choral Pilgrimage for their fortieth anniversary in 2019. 'He's done it again!!!' Harry writes. By which he means, written a masterpiece, and tailored it to the voices of The Sixteen. He sends me a couple of pages; they are in MacMillan's distinctive hand, and Harry highlights both a juicy role for the group's four tenors, whom MacMillan loves, and a meandering, Gaelic-inflected solo line clearly intended for soprano Julie Cooper.

James MacMillan began as something of an *enfant terrible* of contemporary music, provocative and outspoken, prodding the establishment and raging against the machine. But it was never provocation for the sake of it – one sensed a clear mind with a great deal of insight and commitment to his cause, and a certain melancholy at its heart. Over the years, he has mellowed considerably to become one of the elder statesmen of new music. His early works – such as *The Confession of Isobel Gowdie* – revealed an astonishing talent, bold and uncompromising, deftly skilful and vibrantly expressive. His percussion concerto for Evelyn Glennie, *Veni, veni Emanuel*, based on the Advent plainsong, is one of the most frequently performed works of new British music worldwide. He has become a household name, and at the same time lives a local life in Scotland; he has served for many years as organist at his family's Catholic church, penning psalm tunes for them every week, a Bach-like workaday musician. He has also founded his own festival in the East Ayrshire town of his birth, Cumnock, called The Cumnock Tryst, which The Sixteen have visited.

Harry first commissioned Jimmy, as he is widely known, in 2001. Their association has since been a close and fruitful one, bearing works like *O bone Jesu*, *Miserere*, *Stabat Mater* and most recently *O Virgo prudentissima*. A fifth major collaboration is planned for The Sixteen's fortieth-anniversary year, when they will take part in the premiere of a new choral symphony at the Edinburgh International Festival. During our conversation in March, Harry and I discuss the *Miserere* in particular.

Then, in April, The Sixteen travel to Rome to perform the *Stabat Mater* in the Vatican's Sistine Chapel. Exactly a month later, they premiere *O Virgo prudentissima* in the chapel of Eton College, alongside works from the Eton Choirbook. The concerts are live-streamed, and in both cases, an ancient building steeped in presence bears witness to the flowering of a modern masterpiece as it is beamed around the world.

Soon after that Eton concert, Harry and I meet again and discuss the new piece in more detail. We also talk about Genesis Sixteen, Harry's ambitious and transformative project for young musicians, which, like many of the MacMillan commissions, is funded by the Genesis Foundation. What follows is an amalgamation of these two conversations.

ॐ

*This morning I've been listening to Jimmy's* Miserere. *What a remarkable piece, and so very Jimmy. His musical language is so coherent, despite being constructed of very different elements: the Gaelic sound, contemporary choral language – similar to his operatic language – and incense-heavy chords. When did you first encounter his music?*
I think it was probably in the mid-1990s, when his publisher Boosey & Hawkes sent me some of his works to look at. Soon afterwards, we missed out on an opportunity to record his *Seven Last Words from the Cross* because of an exclusive recording contract, but I had wanted to perform his work for a long time. In 2001, Jimmy became the very first composer I commissioned for The Sixteen, with a piece called *O bone Jesu*. Although I had held off commissioning new work partly for financial reasons, it was mainly because there hadn't been a composer until Jimmy I had felt moved to hear from.

*Why is that? What is it about his music that is so enticing for you?*
If you look at the composers through the ages whom I admire, they all have a 'sound' – there's a sound to Monteverdi, a

sound to Purcell, to Palestrina and Sheppard. Britten too has a unique sound. And although I hear a lot of different influences in Jimmy's music, it's absolutely him. What struck me from the very beginning with his music was his knowledge of the scriptures and the texts he was setting, as a devout Catholic. Going back to something we discussed earlier, I've often considered that he's one of the three Catholic composers whose music speaks to me directly: Victoria, Poulenc and MacMillan. His music hits me in the face.

*And you think that's partly because of his personal faith?*
Yes. Of course, his compositional skill is amazing, but it's how he relates it to the text. The *Miserere* theme is from a folk song he wrote, but he reuses it in a totally different guise.

*The* Miserere *is interesting, though, speaking of recognisable themes, because he uses material from the Allegri* Miserere *in reverse, so the major and minor tonalities are switched. It's clear that it's the same music, but it sounds completely different.*
Yes. When I first got the manuscript through in Jimmy's spidery script, and I got to the plainsong bit, my original impression was that he'd run out of ideas. But when you hear it in the context of the piece it is completely new. We talked about this idea with our Genesis Sixteen students a couple of weeks ago. When Jimmy writes for instrumentalists, he has to pack as much information as possible onto each note, but when he's writing for singers, he needs to pare that down, and he very often finds that writing a single word is more effective than any musical markings. At the start of the *Miserere* he marks it 'desolate'. It's immediately clear

from that one word that it has to start incredibly quietly and controlled. The tenors know their breath control has to be amazing. And then he brings in something new, not so much Celtic as Moorish, a wailing soprano and alto motif that sounds to me as if it comes from the hills outside Granada. And it's just so evocative. When he does mark the music '*forte*' he really means it, and you have to dig into your heart and soul to perform it. It's one of the hardest pieces to perform, because it takes every singer to put every ounce of energy into it to make it work.

*I was looking at the page dedicated to the* Miserere *on Boosey & Hawkes' website, and the writer Paul Griffiths describes it as '4 out of 5' ranking in terms of choral difficulty – not because of the notes, but because of how hard it is to pull it off.*
He's right. It's emotionally demanding, but also demanding in the control he wants on those *p* and *pp* markings. We know how to breathe the music now, mainly because of our long association with him. Yes, the soprano duet, with those trills with drones beneath, is tricky, but the most difficult thing is keeping the four-part harmony in tune. It's a challenge to maintain without sinking or rising. Invariably, the piece goes flat when we perform it. It doesn't matter if it goes flat, so long as you've created a performance that communicates the emotion, and the text.

*So how did it come about that you commissioned that first piece from him,* O bone Jesu, *in 2001?*
It began with the Choral Pilgrimage. In our second year, I chose Robert Carver's setting of *O bone Jesu* as the centrepiece

of the programme. I wanted to commission a modern take on the Carver piece. I contacted Jimmy, who was enthusiastic, because it's a really important text for Scottish Catholics, and it meant a lot to him. He told me that his grandfather used to put his head in his hands and say, 'The thing about being Catholic is that you just have to put your head down and get on with it.' Of course, Jimmy isn't quite like that himself.

*He certainly wasn't in the past – he was very outspoken in his early years, and in fact still is today.*
Yes, but of course over the years he has mellowed. He has a lovely sense of humour. His *O bone Jesu* is quite tricky. We talked a lot about voice distribution and range; the sopranos don't like singing top Cs, and the basses don't like bottom Cs. When the score arrived, I looked at it and recognised that he had done everything we'd talked about in writing for The Sixteen. There's a powerful *crescendo* towards the end; in performance people come up afterwards and ask how low the basses are singing and how high the sopranos are singing at the end, but in fact, although it sounds thrilling, they're not higher than a top A or lower than a bottom A.

He often ends pieces with a couple of sopranos on their own, which makes life quite difficult for them – I'm thinking in particular of *The Gallant Weaver*, one of the most beautiful pieces of secular music. My son is having it sung at his wedding. It contains a lot of humming, which is challenging for the singers – but there won't be a single complaint from any of them because it's beautiful music. If it were anyone else, they'd question it, but with Jimmy, he makes us work to achieve it, and when we do achieve it it's so rewarding.

*And although he makes you work, it sits well in the voice, doesn't it?*

Yes, it's demanding but not hard to sing. I remember Jimmy coming down to rehearsals for *O bone Jesu*, and what really impressed him was how hard we worked to make the piece come to life. He was pleased with our dedication, and that doesn't always happen with contemporary music. By his own admission, a lot of his pieces are slow, but within that slow tempo there will always be movement. He's just a staggeringly good composer.

*O bone Jesu* was a huge success. We toured it around the States in 2005, and the response was so positive. Wherever we went, the audience would come out talking not about Tallis, who was also on the programme, but about 'Jimmy Mac', as they called him.

*What was the next piece he wrote for you after* O bone Jesu?

The *Miserere*. That one didn't come from me, but he wrote it for us to perform at a festival in Antwerp. They wanted us to perform the Allegri *Miserere*, and informed me that they'd commissioned Jimmy to write his own setting of the text. When I got his score through, I saw that he had dedicated it to me. I was touched, and four years later I was able to include it in our *Queen of Heaven* Choral Pilgrimage programme. We have had a constant connection with his music, which in recent years has grown and grown. We recorded a disc of his music, including his *Strathclyde Motets* and a full choir version of his *Tenebrae Responsories*. It has been a gradual process of getting to know his music more deeply.

All of the works Jimmy's written for us in recent years have been commissioned by the Genesis Foundation. The Foundation is run by John Studzinski, an inspiring presence in my life and in Jimmy's too. He is a fervent Catholic who donates money not just to the Catholic Church, but also to the fine and performing arts, and various charities working with refugees.

John was behind the commission of the *Stabat Mater*. He had been in Salzburg, and had listened to a performance of Rossini's *Stabat Mater*, and hated it. He texted me after the performance and said: 'We have to do something about this.' He asked me to do some research to find out more about what settings of the *Stabat Mater* text there are, particularly more recent ones. Of course, from earlier centuries there are plenty: Palestrina, Anerio, Josquin, stacks of them in the Eton Choirbook, then later, Pergolesi and Haydn. But more recently, there are only really the settings by Poulenc and Szymanowski – and then by a couple of living composers, such as Karl Jenkins, and a small one by Arvo Pärt. So we thought it was time for a new one, and it was clear there was only one composer who could write it.

*Was it set from the beginning that it would be for voices and instruments?*
Yes, the commission was for The Sixteen with instruments, for us to perform with Britten Sinfonia. Jimmy and I talked about it and decided on having just strings, partly because of his *Seven Last Words from the Cross*, which had been the same scoring about twenty years earlier. Jimmy had previously conducted The Sixteen in a performance of that piece in Holland.

Bit by bit, he sent me through each movement – all of them slow, as to be expected. He used the ending of his own *Seven Last Words from the Cross* as the musical starting-point for the piece; *Seven Last Words from the Cross* ends on a high dyad, and the *Stabat Mater* begins in the same place, very exposed. But Jimmy has progressed so much since the earlier piece. He sets the scene of the event with the orchestra; conjuring the light and the darkness, the blowing of trees, the sand, the expressions of the crowd baying for Christ's death, and those wailing for him, the sight of the mother at the foot of the cross – every aspect of that day is in the piece. He's talked more and more about silence over the years and how powerful it is, and it's there in the music. The fourth movement starts with grovelling, shimmering basses, and then disappears. All the silences in that section are indeterminate. As a conductor, those silences were the hardest thing to control, making those moments special, ensuring I didn't overdo or underplay them.

*Silence is something you've spoken about in relation to Renaissance music too, the repertoire you're drawn to.*
That's where the power of choral music is: in silence. The ringing chord at the end of a phrase or piece of music. You want to preserve that moment. And James often talks with the young composers on Genesis Sixteen about the idea of silence, and letting the chords rest. In a lot of his other music – the *Miserere, O Radiant Dawn*, which is one of the *Strathclyde Motets*, or the *Stabat Mater* – he uses a drone, which is very effective. And he manages to make it sound as though there is more there than you are actually hearing; often, in

his orchestral music, you hear instruments that aren't there, or feel there are other things happening. For example, with the drone, he creates a sound as though there were bagpipes or organs playing in the distance. It's simple, but evocative.

*You have recently performed the* Stabat Mater *in the Sistine Chapel. That must have been quite an experience.*
It was unforgettable. We were there with Britten Sinfonia by permission of the Papal Household and the Pope. There was an invited audience, with a front row made up of Cardinals, and it was live-streamed online. The space was awe-inspiring inside. We all walked through the doorway, stopped and looked, and couldn't look away. The chapel was renovated about fifteen or twenty years ago, and the paintings were restored to their original brightness. My own recollection, from having been there a long time ago, was of a dark chapel, but it wasn't like that at all. We were surrounded by these outstanding works of art, ceiling paintings and altarpiece. The current *maestro di cappella*, the director of music, took me up into the gallery where the choir usually sings. It's a tiny space, and he showed me some graffiti crammed in on the wall; the first name there was Josquin himself, dating right back to the 1500s.

Rehearsing there was also a surprise. I imagined it would be too resonant an acoustic to sing in comfortably, but as soon as we started rehearsing, we realised we would easily fill the building. Even the strings sounded different to the way I expected. Usually in that kind of a space, the double basses would either be too boomy, or disappear into the ether, but they were defined and strong. The choir managed not to over-sing and force the building; instead, it felt like the building was being filled with music. At the start of the third movement, there is an outburst: the choir sings *fff* on its own, followed by silence, and then these filigree soft passages which made the chapel fill with an extraordinary power. We all feel that Jimmy's *Stabat Mater* is a masterpiece, but it took on an extra dimension in this ancient space. By the final movement we were completely drained, it was such an emotionally powerful experience. The old complemented the new, and made it visceral. We were witness to something unique that day, and once again it was thanks to John Studzinski for making it happen.

*John has inspired a number of other commissions for The Sixteen, besides those by Jimmy, hasn't he?*
Yes. We have an ongoing series of projects in which we commission three composers to write short works on the same text or idea. The first of those projects was called 'Padre Pio'. John commissioned three composers – Roxanna Panufnik, Will Todd and James MacMillan – to write settings of the prayer 'Stay with Me, Lord', by Padre Pio, a Capuchin monk [now Saint Pio]. The Sixteen premiered all three works in Westminster Cathedral in June 2008. Every three years, John commissions three composers to set a certain text. The next set of commissions in 2011 was of texts by two Spanish mystics, St Teresa of Avila and St John of the Cross. He asked me to find three composers, and I selected Tarik O'Regan, Ruth Byrchmore and Roderick Williams. And a more recent one was of *Stabat Mater* verses – we called them the 'Mini Maters' – each setting ten minutes long. For that,

we had Alissa Firsova, Tõnu Kõrvits and Matthew Martin. In all cases, the brief was to write for The Sixteen, but to make the music performable enough that most good choirs could manage it, so that it builds the liturgical repertoire.

The most recent has been the Eton Choirbook project, which Jimmy's latest work sat alongside. The three commissioned composers were Marco Galvani, Joseph Phibbs and Phillip Cooke. We asked them to take three short texts from the Eton Choirbook and somehow illuminate this extraordinary music from the 1500s for the modern day. As a side-note, the project was originally connected to the Chapel Royal of St George's Windsor, but it became very difficult to confirm a date, and now we realise why – a certain Royal Wedding [of Prince Harry and Meghan Markle] got in the way. So we transferred the project to Eton, where it sat perfectly.

*We'll come back to that Eton project later on, when we talk about the latest work Jimmy has written for you. But let's carry on with these smaller commissions for now. Who chooses the composers for them?*

In all but the Padre Pio project, which we were brought in on after it had started, John has asked me and Jimmy to recommend the composers. I have asked the likes of James O'Donnell from Westminster Abbey and Andrew Carwood from St Paul's Cathedral to suggest names to me, to help me identify the interesting young voices. And it's alarming how few people they feel able to recommend. That says a lot to me about how small the pool of excellent young choral composers is. It's similar to the pool of singers, in fact. We wanted to find younger composers, or those without publishers, to help promote them.

*And once they are commissioned, how closely do you and The Sixteen work with the composers on their pieces?*
I talk to them initially about the brief, and then John likes to meet them to get a feel for their personalities. And recently, we have used the singers of the Genesis Sixteen scheme as sort of guinea pigs, trying out the pieces to see how singable they are. From the outset, we asked the composers if they would mind having their works taken apart by us – by me, by The Sixteen, and by Jimmy. It was so informative for the composers. With the 'Mini Maters', we workshopped the pieces in London over a weekend during the third Genesis Sixteen course, and it was fascinating. Jimmy gave some overall advice, and then the singers came up with their input, followed by myself and Eamonn Dougan.

*What sort of input?*
Well, as an example, there was recently a composer who wrote in quite a lot of fussy articulation and dynamic markings, and Jimmy asked him if he wrote a lot of orchestral music. He said he did, and Jimmy explained the need to be more sparing with markings for singers. The better the choir, the more instinctive they will be with the musical language, and singers don't need detail spelled out in the same way as orchestral musicians – if they get a feeling for it, detail tends to come more naturally. So when composers write a lot of *tenuto* markings over words, they aren't trusting the singers to follow simple word-stresses, which is common sense. Or

there might be too many breaths marked in the score, which doesn't leave the singers space to find out what works best for them. These are the kinds of things that composers find out through working with us.

*So, let's move on to talking about Genesis Sixteen, which is the extensive education programme you run for young singers and conductors. From its name, it's clear that it too is linked to the Genesis Foundation.*

Yes, it's completely funded by the Foundation. Some years back, when I had already done some projects – commissions and performances – for John, he asked me if there was anything he could do for me in return. I think it was around 2000 that I first became concerned about the lack of people coming into the profession, into the singing world. There seemed to be fewer and fewer people following a similar path to mine, and I was trying to work out why that might be. In my day, and right up to the end of the 1990s, you could get a place at Oxbridge as a choral scholar if you could sing. The academic requirements mattered, but not as much as they do today; if you had a good singing voice, and the choir director wanted you, it was up to your tutor to make sure you got through your degree course. So there used to be people passing through the wonderful Oxbridge singing tradition, singing day in and out, living a privileged existence that doesn't really exist anywhere else in the world, and they were all incredibly talented singers. But now, students are having to get straight As at 'A' level in order to get in to Oxbridge, and the pool of excellent singers within those academic constraints becomes smaller. Of course, there are a lot of universities that offer terrific singing opportunities too, such as York and Durham; but there is nothing quite like the demands of the Oxbridge chapel, where you are having to sing different music every day of the term for three years.

So it seemed to me that there was probably a pool of very talented young singers who perhaps didn't have the academic qualifications to get in to Oxbridge, and I wondered where they were. I wanted to find out, and give them the opportunity to sing at a high standard. And so we started the Genesis Sixteen scheme, with an unwritten rule that we wouldn't offer places to those already in the top Oxbridge choirs, but would try and cast the net wider. John thought it was a great idea, and said he would fund it for three years. We were both very honest at the start, agreeing that if the pilot scheme ended and either one of us thought it hadn't worked, that we would stop there. Of course, it was a huge success, and we have continued it.

Because the scheme is funded entirely by the Genesis Foundation, we are able to offer it completely free to the participants. In this day and age, with huge university fees, that is very important. There are a lot of other courses out there, such as the National Youth Choirs of Great Britain and Eton Choral Courses, but they do cost – there are bursaries too, and I know they are striving to increase them – but I am proud that ours is completely free.

*So who are your singers?*
We've refined the requirements a bit over the years, but it's roughly the same as when we started: the singers must be aged between eighteen and twenty-three, having regular

singing lessons, and contemplating a career in singing. We try to encourage singers from state schools, and we have had a higher percentage of state school applicants over the last couple of years. In the first year, we had over four hundred applications, and that's dropped down to about two hundred a year. We audition up and down the country, with six audition days in London, and one each in Manchester, Cardiff and Glasgow. The scheme is specifically for UK residents, and we have twenty-two places to fill, for a choir of SATB (soprano, alto, tenor and bass).

The scheme is now in its eighth year. When we started it, we involved existing members of The Sixteen in it, which we felt was important. We asked the group who would be interested in being part of the audition panel, and since then Eamonn Dougan and myself have run the audition process together. Singers Julie Cooper, Charlotte Mobbs, Sally Dunkley and Tim Jones have also been on the panel, as they know what we are looking for. We arrange a set aria book for each voice part, with music to suit different ranges. The auditioning singers pick two arias each, and a third of their own choice. We also usually give them some sight-reading. The panel has a simple brief: if they hear something special, either someone very musical, or with real character in their singing, we put a gold star by their name. And there's a blue star for someone we think isn't quite ready but would like to hear again the next year. We have only ten minutes with each singer, but in those ten minutes you learn such a lot about their personalities.

*And what does the course entail?*

We offer a week's intensive residential course at Magdalen, Oxford, in August, then a long weekend in November which is usually in Manchester tied to a concert given by The Sixteen. Then they have a long weekend in February which is usually in London, sometimes further afield; and finally a week's residential course in London in July after the end of the academic year. With those courses we do a very limited repertoire, but very varied – it could be a piece by Josquin, Byrd, Bach, Britten or Tippett, not all of it sacred either – and we go into that repertoire in incredible detail. The mind boggles at how you can spend three hours working on just two pages of music.

The course is taught by Eamonn and myself, and we begin by teaching the whole choir. We then divide them into consorts, led by four members of The Sixteen. We set the repertoire – an English madrigal, a sacred piece, an Italian madrigal – and they come up with their own ideas, developing their one-to-a-part singing.

Then Mary King [vocal teacher and renowned workshop leader] arrives, and she starts off playing theatre games devised by Peter Brook with the young musicians. It begins with a lot of laughter, and ends with absolute concentration, developing their ability to multi-task and to focus. In one game, she has them throw rolled-up socks to one another, and then it builds with more socks, and they realise that in order to succeed at the game they have to have good breath control and flow.

Then she has them work on a more complex piece of music – for example, a Britten *Flower Song* – and she gets them to sit down, and as they're about to sing an entry, they have to rise from their seat. And of course, it's perfect every time, because the mind is being taken on to something other than the complexity of the music.

Then they get a shock of a workshop, delivered by a top ENT [ear, nose and throat] specialist. They get shown rather horrific images of people with nodules or polyps on their vocal cords, people who have screamed too loud for too many years at football matches. It teaches them all about good vocal hygiene and vocal health, which is great for the singers to know. And then there are more practical workshops, for example somebody else might come in and talk to them about tax. As a young singer just starting out in the profession, I wish that someone had told me that you needed to save enough money from your earnings to pay the tax bill. So the Genesis project is about showing these young singers what's possible out there, and how to take care of themselves in the profession.

When we get our final twenty-two singers, we have no idea if they're going to work together. We've chosen them because we think they're special. There may be a voice that's fighting to get out, that's really big. But we talk a lot about supporting each other, feeding off each other, finding a way to blend with the person next to you.

We always begin the first rehearsal with Byrd's communion motet, *Ave verum corpus*. Most of the singers will immediately sing it in the way they think I want to hear it – with a rather bland, Oxbridge sound. I invariably ask them for more warmth. Then I ask them to move about so that they stand in a circle, and scrambled, so they're not standing within their own voice parts. And I make them turn their backs on the circle, so they are facing outwards and can't see each other. I set the beat, the *tactus*, and it's their job to feel it. It is a fascinating process, because they suddenly realise how important it is to feel the beat and listen to one another.

*Do you find that singers from conservatoires are very different from those who are coming through the university or chapel choir system?*

Yes, and what is strong about Genesis Sixteen is the mix. We regularly have singers from York University or Royal Holloway, who have choirs as good as the ones in Oxbridge. The chapel choir singers will tend to be the ones who sing the arch of a phrase, and then make the mistake of tailing away on the last two notes. Whereas the conservatoire singers will sing right to the end of the phrase and put too much emphasis on the final note. It's a question of how to blend the two.

I think it's fair to say that with a lot of conservatoire students the sight-reading is more variable. Many of the choral scholars, or those who have been choristers, have much better sight-reading, but it's interesting putting people who don't read so well with people who do. If you're musical, sight-reading can easily develop, and it doesn't have to be that difficult. I have limited patience for conservatoire teachers who tell their singing students not to sing in a choir. It happens here and in America. It's strange, because if you are studying an instrument, you are encouraged to play in an orchestra, but often singing teachers get this idea that singing in a choir will damage a soloist's voice. If a young singing student in that environment ends up singing in a chamber choir, they will do it without much commitment, and regardless of who runs a chamber choir, if the singers aren't committed it won't be any good. Eamonn is now running a chamber choir at the Guildhall School of Music and Drama in London, and it's part of the curriculum, which is great. The singing teachers are starting to see its benefit. It has a knock-on effect too; if singers are taught to sing in ensembles, they become better soloists. I remember conducting a Mozart Requiem once, and the four soloists who were booked were all big names, but they simply couldn't sing together as a quartet.

We spend a lot of our time on the Genesis Sixteen courses figuring out what the singers need to get rid of. Eamonn is very focused on technique, developing their basic in-breath, how to keep singing on the line of a phrase right the way through. If they don't have good breath control, they run out of it, the sound isn't supported, and the music slips out of tune. We might find a singer who has a very slow wobble, a bad vibrato, which has to be killed instantly; it shouldn't be there in such a young singer, and will develop into a bad habit.

I talk often about an imaginary textbook of choral singing. I find that people approach choral music as though they are following some bizarre rules, and I have to disabuse them of the idea that this book exists. I wonder if they have listened to too many CDs, and think that choral music has to be sung in a particular way. I tell them over and over again: I want to hear your voice, not you singing the way you think I want you to sing. I think it's a new concept for a lot of them, the idea that we are allowing them to sing with their full voices.

*And that, as you've mentioned before, is the approach you have with The Sixteen too. The warmth and clarity of the group's sound can't be achieved by trying to imitate it – those qualities are surely the result of you letting people sing with their own voices, and shaping that sound.*

Yes, and once again it comes back to listening. It's about encouraging the singers to find a way to feed off the person standing next to them. Each individual singer is effectively taking charge of the situation, and not just following a leader. One of the greatest joys of the scheme, for me, is hearing the excitement and the spin in the sound when they realise that. A lot of it comes down to knowing and understanding the text you are singing, and making it sound natural rather than fake.

Over the eight years of doing the Genesis Sixteen auditions, we have learned to identify very quickly where the singers are at. You can see the ones who have fallen prey to the idea of the imaginary textbook, where the words don't seem to have any meaning at all, the phrases are chopped, the voice is constrained, and the natural timbre of it is held back. It points to a musicality fighting to get out. For three weeks of the year, we take that musicality and go into great depth with it. We know it's been a success story, because now we use several of the Genesis Sixteen graduates as deps for The Sixteen itself. We also have feedback from other directors, such as James O'Donnell and Andrew Carwood, that the Genesis graduates are excellent deps. And they have also gone on to form their own ensembles: Fieri Consort, The Gesualdo Six, echo and Recordare are all the results of Genesis Sixteen.

*I'm fascinated by the psychology of the voice. Your description of the moment that they start to use their voices fully, and something clicks, has got me thinking. So has the comment that Jimmy makes about orchestral musicians and singers needing a different kind of information; or Mary King demonstrating that if you take your mind off it, the voice can free up. I'm struck by how much our mental processes get in the way of simply allowing breath and voice to flow – and surely that is a lesson for all singers, not just young professionals?*

You're right; the mind gets in the way all the time. I think it's part of being human. We are all responsible for our own voices, as singers. Much of it also has to do with bedding the music into the voice. In the first rehearsal of Genesis Sixteen courses, the choir always goes out of tune because they don't know the music.

*And when a conductor repeatedly says, 'You're going flat,' it makes it worse.*

Absolutely. The eyebrows raise and everyone tenses up. When singers are tired, it has an impact on the voice. Solid technique is a prerequisite for good ensemble singers. Everybody needs to keep learning, and to go away and work on what they're not succeeding at. It's why I insist that they are having singing lessons, so they can maintain their voices and develop them with the guidance of a teacher.

Listening back is also so important. I remember a number of years ago, the tenor Ian Partridge came to do a workshop with four or five singers on performing as a soloist in English oratorio – Handel and the like. They were great singers, but they all got the shock of their lives to discover that their diction was really poor. And with Genesis Sixteen, we tell them to sing into a mirror. If your face is alive, the music comes alive. If you have a blank face, the sound is actually dull – not just visually dull, but the sound itself has no sheen. Words are fundamentally important, and they need to be produced in the front of the mouth. We do a little technical example during the informal concert at the end of one of the Genesis Sixteen courses. Eamonn gets the students to sing a chord, first without any resonance, then raising their soft palates, keeping their tongues forward and making sure they increase the space between their back molars. The effect of that change is so striking: from a dead, colourless sound to one that is vibrant and ringing.

*It sounds as though the people you bring on the Genesis Sixteen course as tutors – Ian Partridge, Mary King, the ENT specialist, yourself and Eamonn – have a really positive effect on the participants. What about the composers they've worked with?*
Oh, that's been brilliant. When we were working on the 'Mini Mater' series, for example, it was fascinating for the singers to encounter these three very different composers. It makes a real difference for the singers to hear from the composers themselves about what they want. Tõnu Kõrvits, for example, wrote a harmonically tricky piece in an unfamiliar mode, but he played it on the piano for our singers and described how it was based on a South Estonian folk song, and suddenly it made sense to them.

We've brought Jimmy in to teach on the February course on two occasions now. A lot of the students on Genesis Sixteen are composing themselves, as well as singing, or wanting to direct their own ensembles, so it's a very useful process for them. Jimmy spoke to them a lot about how, as a composer, you are constantly searching for simpler ways of achieving the effect you ultimately want. Britten always said that, too; he wanted to rewrite *A Boy was Born* because it was so difficult, and he could have found much simpler ways of achieving the same effects.

*I want to return to James MacMillan before we end, because we talked earlier about three of his works for you –* O bone Jesu, Miserere *and* Stabat Mater *– but we have yet to touch on the newest work he has written for The Sixteen,* O Virgo prudentissima. *You sent me an excited email about it when he sent you the score. What happened next?*

I opened the score and was immediately reminded of how well he knows the group. In the email I sent you, I highlighted the solo he has clearly written for Julie, even though it isn't named; and the part for the four tenors. He has a fascination with our tenor section – Mark Dobell, Simon Berridge, Jeremy Budd and George Pooley – and he wrote a part for four tenors in the *Stabat Mater* too. I mentioned before that Jimmy likes the sound of female voices humming. If that humming is too high, it's extremely difficult for the singers. Jimmy has taken that on board, so instead of writing a hum for the sopranos, he has them sing on 'ng', which opens the throat and stops the sound being constricted. It's simple but makes a huge difference to our singers. In one part of *O Virgo prudentissima*, he has the sopranos and altos singing at different times what is, in effect, like plainsong. It's a sort of melody of its own, with the sopranos singing lengthy phrases, taking them up to a high A flat.

There was one part that caught my eye, which I queried with Jimmy. Towards the end he has written a beautiful melody for sopranos, which sounds typically Celtic. In a funny way it reminds me of the Britten *Serenade for Tenor, Horn and Strings*. He writes a sequence of quick runs which jump up first to an F, then a G, then a top B flat. I thought at first it was for the full soprano section to sing, but then I realised he had written above it that the sopranos should sing it individually, one after another, in quick succession, as a cluster of overlapping lines. It's notated as one long bar, but as a sequence it lasts about twenty bars. The melody is virtuosic and full-voiced, and I wondered if it would sound like a bit of a mess. I rang him, and he assured me it was exactly what he wanted. We tried it out in rehearsal, and it is staggeringly beautiful. And then the men's voices come in with sporadic, strong chords, and the whole piece winds down. You can understand why I wrote to you that 'he's done it again' – it's another masterpiece.

*What was the brief you gave him? Is it based on the Eton Choir-book, like the set of three small commissions that sat alongside it in performance?*
Yes. Jimmy's piece is based on a fragment by Wylkynson which is in the back of the Eton Choirbook, only six bars long. I knew that Wylkynson would speak to his sensibility. So what he's done in *O Virgo prudentissima* is to start with the fragment, mostly hummed, and then let the music gradually build up. He starts to introduce little ideas that stem

from the style of the Eton Choirbook, running quavers and semiquavers which stop and start, and before you know it the music is suddenly full-blown Jimmy.

And then the music evolves, and there's the big climax towards the end which I mentioned, and the music winds down. At the very end, the Wylkynson fragment returns; it has been his starting-point, materialising and then dematerialising, and it frames the piece at its conclusion just before a resounding 'Alleluia'. The amazing thing about Jimmy's music is that it's all ultimately based on a simple harmonic structure – A minor, D minor, C major – but he manages to space the voices in such a way that those chords sound so exciting. I'm flabbergasted by his imagination, how he comes up with ideas and executes them. And however difficult it may look on the page, particularly when it comes to complex tonality, it's always possible for the singers to find their note within a chord.

*He's a working musician, though, and it makes sense he would write music that singers like to sing. Did they have much time to learn it before your first rehearsal?*
Yes, we sent it out to the group about a month before, to give them a chance to look at it first, and we devoted one of our three rehearsals for the concert to working on the piece. While I get to enjoy hearing the music come to life for the first time, the singers in rehearsal are really focused on how to get around the work's complexity. With the humming I mentioned, they had to figure out a way of staggering the breathing on the bar line, rather than within a bar. Humming can sound jolting, but the way they did it made it sound seamless.

*And how much rehearsal did you have in Eton Chapel itself? I remember you talking about needing to find the sound of a building in a short rehearsal slot.*

We rehearsed on the day of the concert, and Jimmy came along. He made very little comment, as he had done when we first sang his *Miserere* for him. Because we've collaborated so well over the years, he knows that he can trust us and push us. The music sounded terrific in the chapel. My memory of it, from when we sang the Eton Choirbook manuscript music there in the 1980s, was that it was quite a dry acoustic. Perhaps we had been standing too far forward in the space, because this time we stood right by the altar and the acoustic felt excellent. The concert itself was very moving, and they brought the Eton Choirbook itself into the chapel and opened it.

*Had Jimmy seen the Eton Choirbook itself before writing the piece?*

No, although I was able to take him to Eton library to see it before the concert. Until about ten years ago, they kept the Choirbook in the chapel itself, and at the end of term they would take it to Barclays Bank and put it in the vault for safekeeping. The least suspicious way of transporting it was in a wheelbarrow. I love the image of this priceless, ancient book being nonchalantly wheeled through the street hidden in a wheelbarrow. I first saw it myself about twenty years ago, when I made an edition of BBC Radio 3's *The Early Music Show* with Christopher Page [scholar and founder/director of Gothic Voices]. It was a thrill to see it again, and to show it to Jimmy, who was stunned by the beauty of the manuscript's illuminations. Wylkynson's name has a motif: a whelk inside the sun.

*And what happens to the piece now?*
We have just recorded it, ahead of next year's Choral Pilgrimage. Even in the short space of time between the concert and the recording, it seems to have opened up and bedded itself into the singers' voices. The sonorities have become richer and bolder. We are learning to tune certain parts of it better. For example, there are points where Jimmy writes simple chords which have to be rock-solid in their tuning, and through experimenting, we have found that the fifths in the chords have to be tuned quite high for it to work. Above all, we are hugely looking forward to it being the centrepiece of next year's Choral Pilgrimage. We have come to love Jimmy's music so deeply, and after the experience of doing his *Miserere* over and over again on that earlier Choral Pilgrimage, we can't wait to perform it more than thirty times across the country. I feel certain that more and more will reveal itself in the music as the journey continues.

# SIX

# America

The Beast from the East makes a welcome retreat, giving way to the beginnings of an insistent heatwave which will dominate the rest of the summer. From now on, Harry makes the journey from Kent to my home in London, bringing gifts for my newborn daughter, and cake for me. As usual, he is generous to a fault. We sit with the garden doors wide open, and turn our attention to America.

It might seem odd that Harry has set me one of the most quintessentially English choral works to listen to for a conversation about America, but he has asked me nevertheless to consider Handel's *Messiah*. Harry has recorded it three times, twice with The Sixteen and once with the Handel and Haydn Society of Boston, and it is his work with that group that sparks our conversation about the choral scene in the United States. I dip into all three recordings for the sake of interest, and each is entirely different, as we will discuss.

In 2009, Harry was appointed Artistic Director of H+H (as they call themselves), a 200-year-old institution with an illustrious history that includes giving the American premieres of choral masterpieces such as *Messiah*, Haydn's *Creation*, the Verdi Requiem and Bach's *St Matthew Passion*. He was charged with building on the work started by Christopher Hogwood, the celebrated English conductor who also founded the Academy of Ancient Music, and was H+H's Artistic Director from 1986 to 2001, during which time he cemented their reputation for being among the finest exponents of historically informed performance on that side of the Atlantic. During Harry's tenure with the group, he has focused very much on honing the sound of the chorus, and together they have performed an acclaimed series of Handel's oratorios, as well as celebrating the group's two-hundredth anniversary in 2015.

Handel's *Messiah* is at the heart of H+H's work; not only is it the first major oratorio they premiered, it is also an annual staple of their concert calendar. In England, *Messiah* is performed at Christmas and Easter, and in America it goes hand in hand with the holiday season in December. When I ask Harry which movement from the two-part oratorio to listen to, he suggests one of two choruses from Part One: 'For unto us a child is born' or 'And He shall purify'. I pick the former, for obvious reasons.

ॐ

*Harry, why have I listened to this chorus, 'For unto us a child is born' in particular? In fact, why both of the ones you chose?*
I just adore them both. I particularly love Handel's imitative writing, and the beauty of the way he shapes the words and phrases. When choruses sing the line 'For unto us a child is born', they always put the stress on the first word, 'For'. But although it makes musical sense, it is completely wrong in terms of the meaning of the sentence. You have to caress that word, rather than bang it out. It has to progress to the words 'a child is born . . . a son is given'. Handel is at his absolute best in the choruses of *Messiah*. The way the voices reach to the words 'Wonderful' and 'Counsellor' is glorious. I often

like to keep choirs on their toes in that movement; if I feel they are starting to sound a bit dull, I will be cheeky and mouth 'Wonderful' when they are meant to be singing 'Counsellor' and vice versa. It seems to work, and stops the music getting stale.

In fact, I've performed *Messiah* over a hundred times with The Sixteen, and it has never felt stale for me. H+H give three performances every year, in November and December. Every time, it's a thrill getting to the end of the piece and the 'Amen' chorus, which I could just as easily have suggested you listen to. It's one of the greatest pieces on one word ever written. It has old-fashioned polyphony in it, inventive phrases with three different patterns going at once, inversions, architectural phrases – it's fantastically written. I conduct it in a very instrumental way, with the singers imagining they are playing a cello, full of articulation but also with long bow-lines. And it doesn't matter how many performances I give of it, my spine shivers every time the sopranos reach the top A climax. I always find something new in Handel's score, no matter how often I come back to it.

Messiah *seems to be at the heart of your work in America. Before you started working with H+H, how much work had you done Stateside?*
I had been on a few tours with The Sixteen, but not much besides that. The tours were sporadic because they lost us so much money. And my only other American experience was conducting two *Messiah* performances, one with the St Louis Symphony Orchestra, the other with the San Francisco Symphony. They were both large choruses, and I found them

malleable, although I was able to do a little more with San Francisco – they were particularly receptive. In those days, I was signed to HarrisonParrott agency, and they felt that doing more work in America would be good for my career. Every American symphony orchestra performs *Messiah* in December. It's rather like people going to Midnight Mass in England – they go because they think they should, and sometimes, for the musicians, it's repetitive, as though they are going through the motions. In both cases, I spent energy trying to get a symphony orchestra to play in a stylish way, even though they are not historically informed ensembles.

*How does one manage that?*
With difficulty. There are some period conductors who make sure the parts, particularly those of the continuo, are heavily marked up. I don't expect symphony orchestras to be able to play in a period style, it's an unfair thing to ask them to do, given the amount and the range of the music they have to be able to play, from Brahms and Mahler to Birtwistle. That's not my way of doing things. I just wanted them to listen to what was happening around them, particularly the continuo, inviting them to really be the bedrock of the group. Their tendency, in the large choruses, was to get stuck in and play *forte*. In the early-music world, it seems obvious to everyone that alternating *forte* and *piano* markings shouldn't be taken literally. But modern orchestras don't always realise it. Those markings are rather an indication to the instrumentalists that the singer is singing (when their parts are marked *piano* so that they don't overwhelm them), or has stopped singing (when their parts revert to *forte*). In

the middle of the aria 'How beautiful are the feet', you're not supposed to suddenly start playing *forte* when the singer stops. There are moments when Handel does, of course, write dynamics for effect, but in general that's a simple rule to follow with baroque music, and I was able to make a bit of headway there.

*What about the singers you came across in the larger American choruses?*

One thing I encountered was that they wanted everything to be written out specifically in their copies. They wanted to know exactly what they needed to do. It was interesting trying to get them to think outside the box of being a chorus; to think dramatically, to think they were part of a narrative taking them right through the Christian year, through so many emotions, to act it and believe it more. That process tended to free them up. I don't think there's any difference between America and England in that respect. I remember doing the Mozart version of *Messiah* with the BBC Philharmonic and Huddersfield Choral Society, and I wanted them to make a really meaty sound, and I asked them for their rawness. I don't really like working with big choruses, because I have my world of smaller consort singing which I so enjoy.

*So, before we talk about H+H, tell me about the recordings of* Messiah *you've done over the years.*

I've recorded *Messiah* three times: once years ago with The Sixteen in about 1985 for Hyperion; again with The Sixteen in 2010 for CORO; and about three or four years ago I did a live recording with H+H, for their two-hundredth anniversary.

My first recording with The Sixteen was in a scaled-down version. That recording marked the start of The Sixteen's band, which has been called The Sixteen Orchestra and also, for a few years, The Symphony of Harmony and Invention. As I think I've mentioned before, in the early days of The Sixteen, we needed to get our name known and make a bit more money, so we teamed up with Ton Koopman's Amsterdam Baroque Orchestra. I gave the choir to Ton to use for various things, first of all a performance of Bach's B minor Mass. For two or three years this went on, and I learned a lot from Ton, who's full of ideas. But we did a big *Messiah* tour, and he recorded it with The Sixteen for Erato, and during that process I was getting itchy feet. I felt also that the choir wasn't really singing the way they wanted to be singing, so it seemed the perfect time to form our own orchestra. I had learned a lot during my time with Ton, particularly from the violinist Monica Huggett, who was the leader of Amsterdam Baroque. So I came back and met up with Ted Perry, the founder and director of the Hyperion record label, and I told him that I wanted to do four live concerts at St John's Smith Square, and that he should record them all live. I was trying it on, really, but Ted said: yes, but I would need an orchestra. I had never conducted *Messiah* before, although I had sung in numerous performances and knew exactly what I wanted to do with it.

So, I formed an orchestra centred round two excellent continuo players: the baroque cellist Jane Coe, who sadly died a few years ago and was principal cello for Trevor Pinnock and The English Concert, and the harpsichordist Paul Nicholson, the ultimate continuo player, who has since become a clergyman. We performed *Messiah* four times in St John's Smith Square, Hyperion recorded it, and it got great reviews. But I find it hard to listen to it today, because it's so pared down. There were sixteen voices in the choir, a very scaled-down orchestra, and young soloists including the bass Mike George, soprano Lynne Dawson and alto David James. We didn't even use a harpsichord for some of the continuo, just a chamber organ.

*Why was it so pared down?*
I suppose it was similar to Ton Koopman's approach, which had influenced me. But the thing that most frustrated me about early-music groups in those days – with the exception of John Eliot Gardiner's Monteverdi Choir and English Baroque Soloists – was that people seemed to concentrate on having lots of stylistic ideas in each movement, but had no interest in how to get from one movement to the next. It was as though there was no drama in *Messiah*, and I had felt that singing it in the Abbey all those years ago.

*And of course it is a highly dramatic work. So, are you talking about the pacing of individual movements, and how words are communicated, or more about the overall dramatic arc of the work and how you get musically from one movement to another?*
All of it, really. I'm talking about having the feeling, when you start the Overture, that you know in that particular performance where you'll be ending when you come to the final 'Worthy is the Lamb' and 'Amen' chorus. And a lot of the pacing has to do with the soloists you've got, working off the strengths of those individuals, and therefore reshaping

the drama accordingly. It's about paying attention to the moment you move from a recitative into an aria, and from an aria into a chorus; how you begin the 'Pifa', the pastoral movement which opens the sequence about the shepherds, which is Handel's way of relaxing the music after the previous movement. Handel, in all his choruses, repeats words over and over again, developing the drama; it's a question of understanding that, and the pacing of it. The word 'Amen' is repeated countless times in the final chorus, but you have to know how you get from start to finish. The music must have ebb and flow, light and shade, and as a conductor it's your job to build the architecture of every movement and of the whole work, taking the audience on a journey.

I learned so much from that early recording. It's interesting to compare it with the next one we did, when I finally decided it was time to re-record it in 2008. Our soloists were Carolyn Sampson, Catherine Wyn-Rogers, Mark Padmore and Christopher Purves, three of whom had been so much a part of the group beginning to define itself. The whole drama of that performance is different. It has a greater intensity, I think. The choral singing and the solo singing are both staggeringly good. Carolyn, Mark and Chris had spent the best part of ten wonderful years in the group, and their personalities had learned to shine through singing with The Sixteen, so when they sang as soloists with us, they were able to shine through even more effectively. The recording process felt like a family coming together, everyone thinking on the same wavelength, and I think that translates to the way it sounds. The players reacted so well to the singers too. I remember asking the members of the band, shortly before we made that recording, whether they would like me to start putting on purely orchestral concerts with them, and they were adamant that they didn't want that. They said they did plenty of that kind of thing with other conductors, but the joy of working with The Sixteen was that they always played with singers, and that it was a great delight for them. The sound on that recording I find really vibrant, it's very special to me.

*I would love to know your take on Handel's choruses and how we perform them, because this is a bit of a bugbear of mine. He is such a great choral composer, to state the obvious; in all his oratorios, the chorus plays an incredibly important role in the unfolding drama. When we think of the choruses in Bach's Passions, we think of the integrated role that they play in the dramatic arc of the story, and yet with* Messiah *we (I mean English musicians) somehow forget that, and the choruses can sound so flabby. Why do English performances of* Messiah *seem to have a heaviness to them, and lack dramatic spontaneity?*
That's exactly what I was talking about in the sense of dramatic momentum. I think it must be because of its continuous performance history. I don't think there's any other piece of that period that has been so constantly in the public eye. Even in Handel's time there were big performances of *Messiah*, and right through Victorian times it was put on by large choruses. I think it was then that it gained that heavy-handed approach, where each individual movement is treated with a kind of reverence, but there is no connection between them. We then had the likes of Thomas Beecham and Malcolm Sargent, who did large-scale orchestrations

which are brilliant in their own way, but change the sound of it. So it's one of those works that has benefited from the early-music movement, because it has been released from that heaviness. It's like buying a house that hasn't changed hands in over 150 years; you start to strip back layers of wall-paper, and take away the cobwebs, and then you can start repainting. Which is how I started, paring it back down, finding the drama underneath, and then giving it a fresh coat of paint.

*Would you say the* Messiah *tradition in America is similar to the English one?*
Yes, I would say so. In England, partly because the 'Hallelu-jah' chorus gained such renown, it has become part of our nation's staple musical diet. And the English legacy has caught on in America, so *Messiah* is now traditionally played around the holiday season in December, as I mentioned. And everybody there stands for the 'Hallelujah' chorus.

*They do? Interesting – I didn't realise that was a tradition out-side England.*
Oh yes, they stand in America without fail – more so than in England. Straight up on their feet the moment it begins.

*So, let's not forget your third* Messiah *recording, with H + H. The performance was recorded live in Symphony Hall in Boston in 2015, as part of the two-hundredth anniversary celebrations of the organisation. When did you first conduct the work with H + H?*
My first encounter with them was in 2007, two years before I took up the post of Artistic Director. I remember it so well.

I struggled with the dramatic arc I've talked about, and the players looked so shocked when I said I wanted to run the end of certain movements into the beginning of the next one. It meant they would have to turn the page early, and it took some time before they let go of wanting to finish a movement and take a pause before starting the next one. My recollection of the chorus is that they sang very well, but I had the feeling that there was a blanket in front of them. By that, I mean that they weren't communicating with the audience at all. They were on automatic pilot, as though nobody was watching them. Over the years I have tried to work out why that happens, and change it.

*Was that 2007* Messiah *your first encounter with them?*
Actually, no, I had met them the year before in 2006, in the Esterházy Palace in Eisenstadt, Austria. It was a rather bizarre event. I was being either naive or stupid, but I didn't realise that when they booked me, it was because they were head-hunting for a new Artistic Director. They had a proper search committee, and meanwhile I had no idea I was being considered. Having said that, back in 2001 somebody from H+H had come over to the UK to talk to me, and told me they were looking for someone to take over when Christopher Hogwood's tenure ended. At that time, it was a pretty short conversation. I had no interest in taking on a job like that, because I felt there was so much going on with The Sixteen, and so much freelance work I was enjoying too. Plus, my children were younger, so I froze at the idea. Grant Llewellyn got the job, and I forgot about it. So after Grant left, they had a couple of years when Roger Norrington stood in as Acting

Artistic Director, and during that period they continued looking.

Anyway, they invited me to conduct them in Eisenstadt. This was the group's first European concert, I think, and we were to perform Haydn symphonies – the Esterházy Palace was one of the places where he lived and worked. I find it extraordinary that they wanted to put their trust for such a prestigious event in someone completely unknown to them, as I was. What's more, I really wasn't a Haydn conductor. I had done two or three Haydn symphonies before with the BBC Philharmonic, and a handful of performances of *The Creation*, but I certainly wasn't well versed in his music. I remember looking at the symphonies they had programmed, and reading some books about Haydn, explaining why he had called these three early symphonies 'Le matin', 'Le midi' and 'Le soir'. And then I got to Esterházy, and I looked up at the ceiling, and there were the three paintings of morning, midday and evening which he had taken as his inspiration, as a way of pleasing Prince Esterházy, his employer. And we performed them in that very same room. It was so exciting. They invited me back once after that to cover an orchestral concert when Roger was unwell, and then they asked me again to do *Messiah* in 2007.

When they offered me the job of Artistic Director two years later, I felt it was time for me to take on a new challenge.

*What was the nature of that challenge?*
I wanted to make an impact, and I knew I could do that with the orchestra, but it was the chorus I was worried about. I had only ever conducted The Sixteen, which had

evolved organically. I always knew what I wanted with them, they were my good friends and we had developed together over the years. But although I'm a conductor who predominantly conducts choral music, I don't really conduct other choirs. I know that sounds odd, but my choral experience was all with The Sixteen, and in performances of repertoire that I felt I could say something about, eras of music I wanted to delve into further.

So when I arrived at H+H, it was to a choir of about forty singers. Christopher Hogwood hadn't paid much attention to the choir, because he had wanted to concentrate on transforming the orchestra from a modern to a period ensemble, and to develop things in a country which is still pretty slow off the ground in terms of historically informed performance. There are various pockets of period music in America and lots of small ensembles, but if you take a broader look at the whole country, there are really only two big ensembles who have proper concert series in proper concert halls. Those are the Philharmonia Baroque Orchestra in California, directed by Nicholas McGegan, and H+H in Boston. So I inherited a large choir of mixed voices, and I was very worried about it. I was particularly worried about the blanket I described before. I wanted to get them to communicate. When I was appointed, the first thing I did was to ask everyone to sing for me. And I was honest with them, that there might be some casualties.

*Who are the singers in the choir?*
They are professional singers. At least, in America that's what they're called, because they're paid for performances.

But they aren't what we'd call professional singers here in the UK, because when I first went, the majority of them weren't earning their principal living from music. Most of them had other professions, and some were music teachers, but they weren't singing as their main job. It's only recently become possible for a singer to make a living – albeit meagre – as an ensemble singer. I went and heard them all sing individually, and it was quite frightening to discover that a lot of them didn't have regular singing lessons. One or two of them told me they hadn't had a singing lesson in twenty-five years. In my opinion, if you call yourself a professional singer, you have to take your art seriously. If your career is not in music and you're just doing this for the love of being part of H+H and getting to perform in Symphony Hall, then you should be thinking again. It was a tough process, and I inevitably made quite a few enemies. I also learned, through that process, that the pool of available singers in America isn't that great. I know I've spoken about the lack of younger singers coming through in the UK, but the pool of talent I'm able to draw on in America is smaller. The whole psychology is different. There are a lot of singers and choruses in America, but the number who can sing in a professional ensemble is relatively few. At least so it seemed.

What happened through that process of auditioning, and being strict on the requirements of having singing lessons and being committed to a professional music career, is that word spread quickly that I wanted people who could really sing. The choir of H+H is called the Chorus, and I rather wish it weren't, because to me that gives the impression that it isn't a choir, it isn't an ensemble, it isn't something special.

*What does 'chorus' mean to you, then?*
Well, here in the UK it has connotations of an amateur chorus, and denotes a large group. It does in America too. And the thing about H+H is that although it performs on the grand scale of Symphony Hall, it is really a chamber choir. I try to refer to them in rehearsals as singers, or as a chamber choir, but not a chorus. Anyway, what happened was that people started coming out of the woodwork, because they realised I was looking for a better standard of singing, and in search of the kind of singers who could deliver stand-out solos in Symphony Hall. There is little better for a singer than the opportunity to do a step-out solo in the B minor Mass in a concert hall like that. The profile is so high. So, bit by bit, more singers emerged, and although there still isn't that large a pool, the standard of our singers is excellent. In fact, I've now almost dug a grave for myself, because the standard is so high that if one of our singers can't do a performance, we have to cast the net as wide as New York to find someone to replace them. It's more of a national pool of talent, which is what the orchestra draws on too.

*And how big is your choir now?*
When we're performing *Messiah*, I use thirty-two voices.

*Which is definitely a chamber choir and not a chorus. So, what have you worked on with them to shape their sound?*
A little anecdote will explain it all. A few years ago, I auditioned and appointed a really good baritone. He sits down in his first rehearsal, gets his pencil out, all ready to mark in all the details, and the man sitting next to him turns to him

and says: 'You're not going to need that. All you need to do is listen.' Over my years of working with them, they have come to know how I work, and got used to it. I have stopped them from writing reams of notes in their copies; all I want them to do is to listen. What I didn't realise until recently is that people in the group think I've started a revolution in the way a choir or ensemble sings. I still find that hard to believe, but I close the season with them in May, and when I come back in November to do *Messiah* with them, they tell me that every other conductor they've worked with tells them to do the opposite of what I ask of them.

*Can you give me an example?*
Well, I talk about the breaths being part of the music. But in America they are trained in a particular way, and they do things by the book, which includes marking in every breath. They are trained to sing in tune, to sing together, to blend, but I want them to go a bit further, to risk a bit – and above all to sing the words. That is one of the principles I hold to firmly with them: I want them to sing the words. I tell them to sing as they speak. With Handel, that has to continue right through the fifth and sixth statement of the same words.

*You talk about the American approach to choral training. Let's start with the positives; what are the greatest strengths of their choral scene, as compared to the British one?*
The difference between the UK and America is that we have five hundred years of a choral tradition, and that is something you can't create overnight. I think the American scene is

younger and newer, but it is underpinned by a tremendous commitment.

I would say the greatest strength lies in the university and college system. Every university has a big chorus. They are very strong on close harmony and barbershop groups, and they make a fantastic sound. Every university has its own scene, and in somewhere like Yale it's just staggeringly good. I remember early on in Boston being asked by Dr Andrew Clark, who runs the music at Harvard, to go to one of his choir rehearsals and share my comments with the students. I was so struck by their commitment. The nature of music in American universities is different to British universities, particularly Oxbridge. In America, the student's day is packed with activities from early in the morning until late, everything from lectures to sport and music. You absolutely have to be at rehearsals. They rehearse a lot, and they perform a lot of music from memory. With a group like The Sixteen we can't afford to do that, because we don't have the time, but it means they can achieve an excellent standard. I noticed other things too about their rehearsals; for example, they scrambled the voice parts, meaning nobody stood next to singers performing the same part, like we do in Genesis Sixteen workshops, and in essence that is a great idea, because it makes people aware of the different parts around them. So there is a rigour to the education these singers get, and their commitment to it is incredible.

In Boston itself, there is a thriving choral scene. There's the choir of Boston University's Marsh Chapel, the chapel choir of Emmanuel Church, who have been performing a Bach cantata every Sunday for over forty years, and Trinity Church, which has seven different choirs alone. Since I started in Boston in 2009, there have been so many new groups starting up: the Renaissance vocal ensemble Blue Heron, run by Scott Metcalf; Skylark, who made their UK debut recently; and the all-female Lorelei Ensemble, who are great and have an accent on contemporary music. Practically all their singers are in H+H, and it's reassuring to see that happening.

But there is a big divide in America between singing in a choir and being a soloist. In extending the reach of the singers we were attracting at H+H, I hope I've started to change that. People from professional opera choruses have started auditioning for me, and I have started to mould the choir as a result. I'm delighted by that transformation, and the fact that H+H, and the wider singing community in Boston, has wanted to come on that journey with me.

*Tell me more about what you perceive to be the difference between the UK and USA.*
I think choral America is a culture shock for anyone coming from the UK, as it was for me. Part of it is down to the fact that here in England, in our world of sacred music, we are lucky enough to have many exquisite buildings to sing in. Our whole concept of a choral sound-world is shaped by and geared towards these fantastic chapels and cathedrals. The moment a young singer has a sense of how music fills a building, they develop a certain choral muscle. In America they don't have that. They have fantastic *a cappella* groups, big choirs, university singers, but I'm not sure that you can teach how it feels to sing into the vast stone space of a cathedral.

And it's not just about the buildings; it's also the repertoire.

Every English cathedral choir performs music from the six-teenth century onwards. In America, there is a singular lack of that earlier repertoire. Not exclusively, but if you look through the programmes of the university or college choirs I was talk-ing about, you see a staple diet of American composers like Aaron Copland, Ned Rorem, Morten Lauridsen, Eric Whitacre. Either that, or people grow up singing in a church, where they stick to simple hymn tunes. There are a few great church choirs who sing polyphony, but there is only one proper choir school in the country, St Thomas Fifth Avenue in New York. As a result, singers don't usually grow up steeped in that tradition of music we are lucky enough to have in England.

*An exception to that is the American composer Nico Muhly, who grew up as an Anglican chorister at Grace Episcopal Church in Providence, Rhode Island. He encountered and fell in love with the music of composers like Orlando Gibbons, and that connection to the English choral tradition is important to him as a musician. But that strikes me as very rare.*

Absolutely. If you're introduced to something early on, you get the bug, and you try to find a way of pursuing it. The late John Scott, who ran the music at St Thomas's, had a lasting impact on many Americans. He was an exceptional musi-cian and choir director, and did great things in New York as he had done previously at St Paul's Cathedral in London. He was brilliant at training boys' voices, and a virtuoso organist. His untimely death shook us all, and I'm sure there are many in America who will go on to pursue choral music as their dream because of him.

[ 163 ]

*So how does that lack of early repertoire, and lack of buildings to sing in, impact the sound that American choirs make?*

Well, I'm generalising, but there is a well-honed, concentrated sound that some American choirs have. All the singers are together, it's perfect and in tune, and they spend a lot of time on warm-up exercises, fine-tuning the sound. I think of it as music in pastel shades – it's impressive, but lacking in vibrancy.

*Are you saying they lack heart?*

Not exactly, but I am trying to point to a difference in the approach to choral music which stems from not having roots in much older music. All my singers with The Sixteen have grown up understanding Renaissance music, and they carry that knowledge and understanding into music from Brahms to the present day. They have an approach to all music which stems from polyphony. I don't think all American choirs have that. If you look at the choral conducting Masters programmes in some of the American universities, they make sure to touch on music by Byrd, but they tell their students the two pieces by Byrd that they have to know (usually *Laudibus in sanctis* and *Ave verum corpus*, which are both relatively short), and they leave it at that. The students are required to know something about those pieces technically, and they might have heard them, but they haven't performed them, and crucially they don't know the range of Byrd's music. The same with Handel; they know *Messiah*, but not the *Chandos Anthems*, *Saul* or *Jephtha*.

Speaking of *Saul*, I have brought along an American choral journal for you to look at. I wanted to show you something of the academic nature of the approach in America. The journal is subscribed to by all sorts of choral singers, but it is incredibly academic, and approaches music from the perspective of analysis. To my mind, that is the wrong place to start from. The article on *Saul* spends an entire page discussing where the continuo should play the chords at the end of a recitative – with the singer, or after he or she has finished – but no time talking about the shape, the drama, the music or the words.

Trying to move the H+H musicians away from thinking academically has been my biggest battle, and I have sort of won it. We recently performed Handel's *Hercules*, and when the chorus sang about jealousy it was absolutely spine-chilling. It was better drama than I think I've achieved with The Sixteen, in many ways.

*So how did you achieve that with the H + H singers?*
First and foremost, I talked to them about their body language, and encouraged them to support each other. The group's body language was not good when I first arrived. As well as the imaginary blanket in front of them, they weren't communicating with each other either. They turned away from each other, which I think is how they are taught to sing. Bit by bit, I've encouraged them to get involved in the words and the drama, with their voices and their bodies, and to notice one another. There are some members of the choir who are so, so musical, they get it right away. I have to feed off those people. And these are the same lessons I have to teach the students of Genesis Sixteen.

*That sounds time-consuming. How much rehearsal do you have with H+H?*
Not all that much, so I batter them with information very quickly, and the moment I notice they are tired, I stop. I take risks, so sometimes I won't cover a *Messiah* chorus in the rehearsal, and then I will just go for it in performance. In the first few years, I couldn't afford to be spontaneous, because I had to make sure I had everything covered and wasn't in a position to take those kinds of risks. But a few years in, I realised I didn't have to do exactly the same in performance as I had done in rehearsal. That is a joy for me, and for them too.

So much of the time, with other groups, these singers are being asked to sing exactly what's in their copies every time. It's the same with the instrumentalists too. As I said earlier, they are constantly writing things in their copies, and instead I am asking them to watch me, to get the shape of the music, and to bring it alive in the concert.

The first time I had the choir sing through a piece by Byrd, it sounded completely anaemic, and I shouted at them that I wanted to hear *them* sing. In some ways, it goes back to that imaginary textbook of choral music I mentioned the other day – this idea singers have of how choral music is 'supposed' to sound.

*Have you found the American imaginary textbook to be the same as the British one?*
Yes, and that's because in the 1970s and '80s, a number of American scholars came over and sat in on rehearsals and concerts for The Sixteen and other English choirs, and

cathedrals, and they took notes. They went on to write their dissertations on the English choral tradition, and that has informed the academic discourse. In America, as I said earlier, choral music is rooted in universities. One's whole education is led by the masters and doctorate programmes; one can't be a tutor unless one has a doctorate. So consequently – and this is a wild generalisation – you're not getting performers and artists training students, therefore everything is academic and led by analysis. Even the programme notes in H+H's booklets were entirely analysis-based when I arrived.

*Did the audiences want that, though?*
I certainly hope not, because I have changed that now. Personally, I think one wants to know the history and colour of a piece of music. Let's say you're about to hear Handel's *Coronation Anthems*. I don't think you want to know the key of the music in bar four. I think you want to know that the Coronation [of King George II and Queen Caroline in 1727] was delayed by two weeks for fear of the Thames flooding; or that during the service, the musicians started playing two different anthems, and, as the Archbishop wrote, 'cacophony ensued'. That's far more interesting to me.

*From my perspective as a broadcaster, whose job it is to give listeners details about the music to inspire them in their listening, I'm inclined to agree with you. But Harry, I'm getting the sense that there were things you encountered with H+H that you didn't like, and that you wanted to change. Were there positives too, rather than challenges, that attracted you to the job?*
Oh, absolutely. I had met many of the players and I really

liked them. There was a very good feeling about the group. And while I didn't know much about the organisation at first, I discovered so much about their history that I admired. They are more than two hundred years old, and there is no other group in the world like them. I made a point of performing *Messiah* in every one of my first eight seasons, because I loved the idea of bringing new life to such an old tradition. I'm so happy to hear from audience members nowadays who say that *Messiah* seems to them like a short piece, whereas it used to feel like a long one. That isn't because we perform it fast, or have cut any of it – it's because the drama moves.

*That must be so satisfying.*
It is. Last year was especially satisfying. I got a great team of soloists together: soprano Katherine Watson, mezzo-soprano Christine Rice, tenor Allan Clayton and baritone Sumner Thompson. The audience got completely wrapped up in the drama, as did the chorus. I particularly remember the sequence from the start of Part Two, when the drama begins to unfold. The viciousness of the chorus 'He trusted in God', and the build-up of that sequence, and then the rest of the tenor solo, 'Thy rebuke' – it was magical, and I was so pleased with the choir.

There have been many highlights of working with H+H. We did a performance of Henry Purcell's *The Fairy Queen* with eighteen singers, and once again I had to encourage them to enjoy the fun, the wit and the emotion of Purcell's music. I got them to let go of the feeling that they had to sit still as classical musicians, that only the maestro on the podium is supposed to have an expressive face. And the music was so exciting and vibrant as a result. I suggested a few ideas, and they ran with it.

*Has working with H + H changed you as a person, as a musician?*
Yes. One of the big discoveries for me as a musician has been Haydn. I'm recording a series of Haydn symphonies with them at the moment, and it has been a complete revelation to me. I said the other day that all orchestral music is new to me; and I'm not ashamed to say that I had no idea Haydn was quite so interesting outside his oratorios. The wit, the imagery in his symphonies is amazing; he can be so pictorial with an orchestra. Of course, you can't get more pictorial than *The Creation* or *The Seasons*, but it's been fascinating to discover that the symphonies are the same.

And I suppose it has made me not want to take The Sixteen for granted. It has also made me drive them to do better too. When I started at H+H, I would come back from Boston and feel a little deflated, and work with The Sixteen and think how lucky I was that they were all on my wavelength. As things have developed with H+H, I've found myself returning to The Sixteen and thinking they seem a bit complacent in the face of the commitment I encounter in America. I feel a real sense of achievement about my time there, and when I leave I will miss it.

*We haven't really spoken about your recordings with H + H . . .*
H+H had very little recording catalogue when I arrived. In Christopher Hogwood's day, he was really busy training up his musicians to play on period instruments, focusing on

that. For such a famous society I felt they needed to start a good recording catalogue. We decided to make a Christmas disc, and this was quite a daunting prospect, because the chorus was only just beginning to take shape. But they had a deal with Boston's public radio station, WGBH. They have a fantastic studio, but one in which all the details of the sound are exposed. It's not like recording in a church. And the singers weren't used to doing recordings like The Sixteen are. Having the microphones up in front of them made them very stiff, so I kept inviting the singers to come into the booth and listen back to themselves.

*How did you choose the repertoire for that Christmas disc?*
I wrote to a lot of people running choirs in Washington, New York, Boston and on the West Coast, and asked them what American motets they performed regularly at Christmas. I was surprised to find that a lot of it was English, music by Herbert Howells or John Rutter. John Scott recommended a piece by James Bassi called *O quem pastores*, which has a barbershop feel to it, and also a lovely little carol by Charles Ives. But the rest were English, like Bob Chilcott's *Shepherd's Carol,* and Robert Pearsall's setting of *In dulci jubilo.* And the carols have the same words to the ones we sing in England, but some have different tunes – pure Victoriana.

*Another disc you recorded with H + H is called* The Old Colony Collection. *That's a fascinating programme. How did you put it together?*
When H+H started, it was also a publishing company, and they put out books on how to sight-read, how to sing, as

well as collections of anthems. It was only during the run-up to the bicentennial that these beautiful old volumes came to my attention, with leather bindings, often falling to pieces. In researching this disc, my hands were constantly covered in leather dust. The volumes came out every two years, and each time a couple of pieces would be added or taken away, but it was mostly the same stuff. For our recording, I sought out some of their collections from the 1820s, early on in the group's life. H+H were part of a movement to get European classical music popularised in America. They even commissioned Beethoven, although he died before he could fulfil it.

*And what sort of repertoire is in those publications?*
They are full of choruses from oratorios by Handel and Haydn, of course, but often marked up for organ, in a rather Romantic style. There's one little piece by Mozart, a four-voice choral version of the aria 'O Isis und Osiris' from *The Magic Flute*, but to religious words. But other than that, it's mostly English composers from the cathedral tradition of the early nineteenth century, from James Kent to Samuel Webbe, mostly verse anthems which were simple enough for the then singers of H+H to tackle.

There's a charming bit in the book on how to sing, which explains musical intervals and how to pitch a note, and then there's a description of the 'tuning break'. This was a break during their rehearsals when they would go downstairs and have a sip of brandy, in order to improve their voices for the second half. And if you look at the H+H accounts from back then, you can see a note of their supply of brandy.

*That is very charming, and I hope you have reintroduced that tradition . . . Speaking of tradition, did you feel it a pressure when you started at H + H?*

Not really, because I saw my job as continuing a new tradition which Christopher Hogwood had started, rather than preserving the old. And although we think of the tradition of H+H as old, we have to remember that when they started, they were interested in the new. At least, Haydn was new, even if Handel was old. And my job is to keep all that music sounding fresh. It is startling for audiences when they hear this music performed with real vibrancy by a period orchestra.

*You are clearly very connected with the audiences of The Sixteen – you speak about them and their reactions to your Choral Pilgrimage concerts a lot. What about the American audience – who are they, and what are they like?*

They are incredible. They are mostly of the older generation, and they all give a huge amount of money and time to the organisation, which helps keep it afloat. We are doing well at attracting younger listeners, but that's still an ongoing project. The audiences at concerts go absolutely wild. It's the norm to have a standing ovation – it's the Boston way. Of course, there is always the danger that a guaranteed ovation means your musicians become satisfied with mediocrity, but I have fantastic musicians to work with, and the audiences have really responded to our improvement. I'm also so impressed by how much the audience knows about music. They are particularly knowledgeable when it comes to Bach, Haydn and Beethoven. Funnily enough, they are less familiar with Handel, and I'm still introducing Handel oratorios to them which they've not heard before.

*Did you have a programme of Handel oratorios in mind when you started?*
Yes. So far, we have performed *Samson, Saul, Jephtha, Semele, Hercules* and *Israel in Egypt* together, and *Belshazzar* is next. I have made a point of only performing the Handel oratorios which I have also conducted in staged versions, because it's only when you put something on stage that you really understand the drama of it, and recognise its relevance to us as modern listeners.

*Do you talk to the performers when you're rehearsing the oratorios for a concert about what you've learned from the staging?*
Yes. I try to get a cast of soloists who have done it with me at some point already. When we did *Saul*, for example, I brought in an entire cast I had worked with before, and the chorus and orchestra were transfixed by the electric drama crossing the stage in the way the soloists performed. They reacted to that brilliantly, and followed suit. I try to make sure the instrumentalists and choir members listen to the way the soloists deliver the text and the story, and keep that energy going. We recently performed *Hercules*, and it was the same; the choruses were terrifying.

*You clearly admire Handel's music. We touched on it with* Messiah *earlier, but may I finish by asking you to pinpoint what it is you so love about his music?*
I think it's the way he creates brilliant drama out of the

simplest of ideas. Think of an aria like 'Total eclipse', from *Samson*. The orchestra plays in unison, and it is captivating. It all stems from his sense of the text, which for a non-native speaker is remarkable. Handel also delves deep into his characters. To me, *Saul* is all about the protagonist's increasing madness, and Handel finds musical ways to drive that madness forwards, for example where he brings in the carillon with the chorus, making him even more enraged. In *Hercules*, the drama is all centred on Dejanira, who goes through agony about inadvertently killing him. And so it goes on, every one of the oratorios centring on real human drama. It's just thrilling music.

# SEVEN
# Conducting

A few days before our next meeting, I sit down at my computer during a rare moment of peace to transcribe our previous conversation about America. My daughter is just a few weeks old and lies beside me in a Moses basket, asleep on her back. As I turn to look at her, her arms suddenly rise up in an involuntary reflex; but rather than floating slowly back down to her side, as they have done before, they stay frozen mid-flight, perpendicular to her body. They remain there for the rest of her nap. Her hands, far from rigid, carry the elegant gesture of an upbeat, and it seems as though she is sculpting air. I call it her 'conductor' pose, and it makes several repeat appearances over the coming days; each time, I delight in imagining the music she might be ushering into existence.

Conducting is a curious art, and much has been written about its development over the centuries, from the French baroque composer Jean-Baptiste Lully famously stamping the ground with a gilded staff, to the enigma of the modern maestro. In a cursory search of the internet, I find several photographs of Harry in elegant evening dress, his arms raised in front of him, eyes bright, conveying the sonic dynamism of the captured moment. In our previous conversations, Harry has spoken a great deal about his general approach to conducting, but primarily in terms of his rehearsal style and the kind of direction he gives his singers.

I want to find out more about how it feels to him to be a conductor of choral and orchestral music, standing in front of musicians waving his arms; and to hear his take on the unique challenges of his profession.

For my listening, Harry has chosen music by another composer close to his heart whom we have yet to discuss: Michael Tippett. The 'Five Spirituals' he has picked out are Tippett's most popular choral works. They come from his searing post-war oratorio, *A Child of our Time*, and from the perspective of Harry's interest in dramatic pacing, they provide five focused moments of collective lament within the harsh fury of the larger work. As a stand-alone group, they are most remarkable for the way in which Tippett appropriates the material of the African-American spirituals for a classically trained choir with four oratorio soloists, and threads them into a cloth of contemporary polyphony without ever stripping them of their original power. Harry strikes an elegant balance in his recording with The Sixteen between Tippett's stark unison lines, bouncing cross-rhythms, occasional outbursts of communal cry, and the consolation of those few moments of pillowy rest.

*When did you first sing the Tippett Spirituals?*
It was with the BBC Singers. Shortly beforehand, Tippett himself had conducted them with the Singers, and I'm sad that I came after that moment. I remember people saying that he had asked for the low basses to 'grumble away' in his setting of 'Nobody Knows', for effect. I love the five pieces,

and we often use them in our Genesis Sixteen courses. I have chosen them for you to listen to because they point to something I think is important, as a conductor, and that is how you read the information in a score.

When I first recorded the Spirituals, on the same disc as our recording of Stravinsky's *Symphony of Psalms*, I decided to phone Tippett up to ask for his advice. He was very ill at the time, and I wasn't able to speak to him directly, so I went through his personal assistant, Meirion Bowen. I wanted to hear from Tippett himself because of a recent experience I had had with Britten's music. I had just recorded a number of Britten's works, including the *Festival Te Deum*, and I realised that although Britten was a contemporary composer, a tradition had already developed around his music, a received way of interpreting his markings. In a piece like the *Hymn to St Cecilia*, nobody uses Britten's metronome markings. But if you actually sing what Britten wrote, as he intended it, the music sounds brilliant – the soprano solo has breath and air and space. So I thought that I would ask Tippett if he had noticed any bad habits springing up in recent performances of his own music, and whether he could advise me on how to perform the Spirituals as he had envisioned them.

*So, what did he say?*
He sent back a note through the fax machine – I still have it somewhere, on Gestetner paper – saying yes, there were all sorts of ways he had heard people sing the Spirituals which were not what he had intended, and he went on to give me several really useful tips. For example, in 'Deep River', he

talked about the very end, the words 'Lord, Lord'. He said that everyone turns that moment into a big *rallentando*, and holds the chord at the end, but he wanted the final notes to disappear, as though a child had gone on bended knees, the prayer simply tailing off. He also spoke about the diaphanous solo soprano line, and that the *pianissimo* he had written there was best performed by Jessye Norman. He also wanted the *crescendi* in 'Steal Away' to be massive.

So, when we came to record them, I took all those pointers on board, and observed all of his tempo markings as well. When we perform the Spirituals, I make sure the four soloists are very much at the front, like a quartet of Evangelists, separated out from the rest of the choir rather than embedded within it. I encourage them to let rip, because it's all about them, as though they have a backing group behind them, nudging the accents. That's another thing Tippett wanted – for his accents to be nudged rather than bashed. And for the vowels to be really long, that's also important.

In 'Deep River', the soprano cascades over the top of the choir and lingers after the line 'walk into Heaven'; the upbeat quaver which leads into the main choir is incredibly hard to achieve unless you lengthen all the vowels, and give the music a cavernous length and breadth. That's something The Sixteen are really good at, singing right through the phrase. Also, you have to do exactly what Tippett says at the start. At the opening of the first stave, the sopranos, altos and tenors have a small *crescendo*, but the basses have a long one. Most conductors try to make everyone crescendo together, but if you do exactly what he writes, the rest of the choir has to listen to the basses, and melt with them onto the next chord, and the music works so much better. You have to allow the ebb and flow of the music, the give and take – if you can't master that, then your choral singing becomes constricted.

*You have talked before about putting your interpretive stamp on music. Generally speaking, are you the kind of conductor who takes the score as gospel?*

Yes, pretty much so. It does depend on the period of music, though. With a Handel oratorio, I will invariably go back to what he first wrote, because that's usually what he really wanted. When I'm dealing with early music, I rely on good editions – that is crucial. I was brought up, as I've talked about before, on David Wulstan's editions that were transposed up a minor third. Sally Dunkley has more recently prepared all my new editions, at original pitch, and the music takes on a new tone colour. Martyn Imrie prepares my Palestrina and Victoria editions, and I know I can rely on them all. I also tend to prefer things to appear in flat keys rather than sharp keys; I don't know exactly why, but it seems they suit us better as singers. I'm not generally pedantic about what keys we do things in, and there are certain pieces which should probably be for male voices, but we decide we want to perform them with SATB choir, so we put them into a key which works for us. John Milsom is also refreshing, and a great help with those sorts of things. We don't really know where singers in the Renaissance got their starting notes from, so a lot of it is guesswork.

*So, for the rest of the morning, we are going to focus on what it means to be a conductor, and your experience of the job. Let's start with the broadest possible question: what is the role of a conductor, in your opinion?*

Primarily, the role of a conductor is to get the best out of the singers and instrumentalists in front of them. When you meet a new group for the first time, through the rehearsal process you have to find a two-way trust: for them to have faith in what you're saying, and for you to trust them to be musicians. Many people would disagree, but I believe that however much work you do in rehearsal, you still have to bring something extra to a performance. Perhaps that is more the case with The Sixteen and H+H, because we know each other so well and can afford to take risks. I love conducting, and I try to be expressive and relaxed, and not to put my singers under vast amounts of stress. I think as a result they like singing for me, and I love conducting them.

*Did you ever have any conducting lessons?*
No, never. I'm completely self-taught.

*How did you learn? I mean, a lot of conducting comes down to individual talent, but there are still techniques to master.*
I learned by watching. I've often asked my singers to pop up and keep conducting while I go out into the auditorium to listen during a rehearsal, and it's interesting how hard some of them find it; it's not just a question of waving your arms. I did do a little bit of conducting at school, but principally I started having a go at university. Bernard Rose in Magdalen Chapel used to want a singer on the opposite side of the chapel to him to mirror his beat, and it was usually me, so I

had to learn how to feel a beat in my wrist for responses and psalms. And then gradually I just got the bug for it.

*Did you conduct into a mirror ever?*
No, I don't think I did. I just watched other people at first. Some of them I admired, but I also learned from people I didn't think were that good, people who didn't really know what to do with their hands. I was lucky to meet people who inspired me. Allan Wicks was certainly one of those, and there is an element of him in my beat. Both Allan and Bernard Rose spoke against mirror-beating, which I've mentioned before – the choral world is full of it. I made lots of my own mistakes, conducting choirs, and bit by bit I started doing things with orchestras too and learning there.

But as I said when we talked about the BBC Singers, that is where I think my conducting really developed, because I watched those conductors like a hawk. I was fascinated by Ozawa's electric beat, in which everything was so, so clear. Rozhdestvensky's enormous beat could also be minimal at times, but there was always rhythm there. And even with Boulez's mirror beat, there was rhythm and musicality.

I have found certain pieces of criticism really useful too, and tried to take them on board. I did a concert with the Academy of St Martin in the Fields some time ago, and one of the orchestral players asked me to use my body less. He said that when I got excited, I moved too much and the beat wasn't clear. I try to encourage that sort of feedback, and I always ask musicians to tell me if I'm not being clear. In coffee breaks and after rehearsals, I talk to the singers and players I have a relationship with.

*So developing that rapport with your players is an important part of conducting?*

Oh absolutely, yes. I remember someone years ago saying to me that as a conductor I always had to connect with the back row of the second violins; even for just a moment, in a concert, so that they know you are connected with them. It's very important.

*How would you describe your own style of conducting?*

I would say I spend a lot of time focusing on the arches of phrases. Practically speaking, more often than not the left hand articulates and shapes a phrase, while the right hand keeps time. Choral music and orchestral music are slightly different in that respect, as are different styles of music. When I was conducting Stravinsky's *Symphony of Psalms*, and recording it with the BBC Philharmonic, I needed to be absolutely clear and rhythmic, minimising my gestures, and from that starting-point I was able to be more spontaneous. I often stretch and point with my left hand to what I think is important, and want to bring out in the music. But then, with Renaissance vocal music, I'm not so rhythmic, certainly not led by the bar lines. Instead, I go with the shape of the words and the phrase. Even Britten's *Sacred and Profane*, where you have to be clear with the rhythm, you can still give a sense of the word stresses and the phrase so that you don't get bogged down in the rhythm. All the time, you need to be physically grounded, and there always has to be rhythm in your body, even when your gestures are small. The more intricate the music is rhythmically – I'm thinking of something like Byrd's *This Day Christ Was Born* – the more I bounce my beat, never letting it get too big. I only use a gesture when the music or the singers really need it.

*Is there a much of a practical difference between conducting orchestras and choirs?*

There shouldn't be really, and I try to encourage my Genesis conductors to get orchestral experience. I used to think I had to be clearer with orchestras than with choirs, but the most important thing with both is breathing. That goes back to Allan Wicks again, who was always talking about breath and preparation, that process of being there and breathing with the music. Wind players have to breathe just the same as singers. If you hold your breath, there's tension in your mouthpiece. It's exactly the same process. Orchestras tend not to be very good at breathing; period orchestras are good, but suddenly when period orchestras get into classical repertoire they get confined by the bar line and they stop breathing. With Baroque music, the players know the music goes with the shape and architecture of the words, but it often begins to get more formulaic from Haydn and Mozart and on to Beethoven. Somehow the musicians get more straitjacketed, and don't breathe as much. I love conducting all these Haydn symphonies I'm doing with H+H, and there's a visceral energy particularly in those faster movements, but I think one of the important things – luckily one of the things I'm good at – is conducting really slowly. I've always made a point of doing Mozart slow movements not in 6 but in a slow 2, but all the while keeping the flow and not allowing the music to stagnate.

*We're starting to get to the heart of something here, Harry. I have been troubled by a theme that's cropped up in our conversations. Whenever I ask you if you had a clear plan of how you wanted things to happen in your life, you answer that things have just unfolded without you really having to do anything. You give the impression of being incredibly laid-back, which seems so unusual for someone with such a successful career. But perhaps that laid-back attitude is your unique style, and related to what it takes to be a good conductor. You have to have an internal sense of relaxation, because if you are tense and wound up, it will wind up the music too.*

You're absolutely right. If a conductor is tense, you can feel it in the music. Again, it reminds me of what I said earlier about Allan Wicks, how he used to turn a mistake during Evensong into something really special. If there's a mistake in one of my concerts, I want my musicians to get over it, and not let it affect them. Often, my singers worry that I will be furious with them, but I won't – I simply smile about it.

*Don't you ever get furious with your singers?*

Occasionally I get a bit quiet, or stop a rehearsal, but very rarely. I suppose, for me, the worst thing is not being able to connect with a performer during a concert. When you're looking at somebody and you can't get their attention, either because they don't want to make eye contact, or because they're just miles away, it feels terrible. If I find during a concert that I'm losing touch with someone, I will do whatever I can to get them back and connect with them again, and I always look back a bar later to make sure their eyes are still on me. It has to be a two-way thing the whole time, the

[ 184 ]

feeling that you are getting some kind of physicality out of their singing and playing as well.

*What's that experience like for you? I've sung for conductors before but have no idea what the eye contact feels like in the other direction.*

It's brilliant. With The Sixteen, it's also kept alive by the behind-the-scenes camaraderie. In our concert the other week in the Sistine Chapel, I had one of those experiences of sheer magic. For that moment, I was in another world, at one with the music and at one with the musicians in front of me. You can only really judge that kind of thing at the end, particularly when the piece ends and you can hold the final moment, and you take it all in, realising that you have been part of something special. I adore it. I love bringing the best out of the people in front of me, and I get frustrated when it doesn't happen. And that's partly why I so rarely conduct other choirs. The Sixteen is such an important part of my life, as is H+H, and I want to be working at that kind of standard, feeling as though everyone is giving of themselves. I often say to my musicians that we are fundamentally entertainers. We are there to make the people who've paid to see us feel better about things. The Choral Pilgrimage is so wonderfully rewarding precisely because of the people we perform to.

*Are you really just providing entertainment? Isn't music supposed to be profound and life-changing too?*

Oh yes, of course. Sorry, I wasn't being flippant; I think the two absolutely go hand in hand. The music we perform on the Choral Pilgrimage is uplifting, and with some of those works, we get so involved and wound up in them. Every performance is so incredibly different. With Jimmy's *Stabat Mater*, I know we found every single performance totally draining, and Sheppard's *Media vita*, which is nearly twenty minutes long, is exhausting for the singers.

This is possibly a fault of mine, but I do worry a lot about how tired my singers might be. I try to make the whole experience less tiring for them; perhaps I should let them suffer more. I try to keep things as relaxed as possible, not just in concerts but also in recording sessions. That was in my mind when we recorded Jimmy's new piece the other week, knowing that some conductors waste a lot of time in recordings because they know they can re-take something. I think when you waste time, you don't get the best out of the people you're working with, and the danger is that conductors wind their artists up. I don't want that at all, particularly not with singers. The voice is so much a part of yourself, if you're wound up or tense, you won't get good results. I know my singers so well, I know just how far I can push them when I need to, because most of the time they know what I want, and give me their all, which makes it exciting and rewarding.

*Can we go back to the difference between orchestral musicians and singers for a moment? I remember you saying the other day that they need different amounts of information in their scores. Is there also a difference between what orchestras and choirs need from a conductor?*

I don't think so, not really. I often talk to singers using instrumental language about phrasing, and conversely I talk to orchestras using the language of singing. Most orchestras regard me as a choral conductor who doesn't know much about orchestral music, I think. That was certainly the case when I started at H+H; but they soon realised I had actually conducted quite a lot of modern orchestras, not just the period band of The Sixteen.

For me, the delight of conducting an orchestra is, as I've said before, that I am coming to the music for the first time. I don't listen to a lot of recorded music, and I don't count myself an academic or get bogged down in books, so I come fresh.

*Yes, you mentioned that particularly in relation to Haydn the other day. I have to say, I was a little surprised by that, not that it was true, but that you so happily admitted it. There's often this idea that the conductor needs to be the authority on music, and know the orchestral repertoire inside out. It takes quite a lot of courage and self-belief to be honest about your innocence, in a way, and know that it benefits your work.*

Yes, and I think with my work at H+H, they have come to realise that I have a fresh approach, and they appreciate it. Of course, I always know the music I'm conducting at any given time, and I prepare myself very well. I think it's quite a fine balance. When you hear great conductors who are authorities on music and have an in-depth knowledge of the repertoire – and this applies to opera conductors too – they come with a lot of preconceived ideas. It's as though they know what it will sound like before they've begun. I think for instrumentalists and singers, my approach is refreshing. I tend to talk to them in pictorial terms. I was fascinated to learn that both Georg

Solti and Nikolaus Harnoncourt spoke in pictorial terms to their musicians too. Reading that gave me the courage to do the same. There are, of course, areas of music I shy away from, because I don't feel I know the music enough to conduct it. I don't do Beethoven, for example; I just really don't think it's 'me', I don't feel comfortable in it, and there are thousands of people out there who can do it better.

*I'm glad you just mentioned two great conductors, Solti and Harnoncourt, because I wanted to ask you about the other conductors who have inspired you. You've also touched on Ozawa, Boulez and Rozhdestvensky from your time at the BBC Singers, and of course Allan Wicks early on. Were there any others?*
Yes, Leonard Bernstein. At home, in the family room, we always had the television on, and I remember once seeing a live broadcast of the Verdi Requiem from St Paul's Cathedral. I was about sixteen years old, Bernstein was conducting, and I was gobsmacked by his electricity. He seemed to be oozing music, or taking the music that was coming at him from a big chorus and orchestra, taking it into himself, and somehow exuding it from his body to everyone who was listening there, and there I was watching him on the black-and-white television. I was absolutely fascinated by the whole thing, even though I knew nothing about him.

*It's interesting that it was Bernstein's actual conducting, rather than his persona and role as an educator, which first inspired you.*
Yes, I suppose that's true. Years later I bought his recording of Haydn's *Creation*, and I remember thinking how natural his feel for the music was. His tempi were pretty similar to

those of a period orchestra, and somehow his sheer musicianship carried the whole piece through. He was such a showman too.

*You also said you learned a lot from the less good conductors. Without naming any names, what were their faults that you learned to avoid?*
For me, bad rehearsing and bad conducting go hand in hand. There were some people I sang for who would over-rehearse. It would get to five minutes before the end of our allotted rehearsal time, and they would be going over something again and again. We were all excellent sight-readers, and didn't need to learn the notes, and they weren't really saying anything new about the music, so it seemed that they were just going over it to learn it themselves. That really used to annoy me, because a conductor should come prepared. The conductor cannot be learning the music through the rehearsal process. My group would be stunned if I didn't know what was coming next when I turned a page.

I also had little patience for conductors who rehearsed, and then had nothing more to say in performance. You have to give something more. Another fault I found was with people who blatantly ignored a composer's indication in a score. Or, conversely, those who followed the score so mechanically that it put the music in a straitjacket, and it stopped having any meaning as music. Others would come in and focus in on one tiny detail for ages, completely ignoring the places where the singers were floundering. Or, as I mentioned before, the tendency in larger-scale works to compartmentalise every movement, rather than seeing through the dramatic arc of the piece. Those are all things I have been careful to avoid myself.

*So, having been a singer and on the receiving end of bad conducting has shaped you as a conductor.*
Yes. I was talking earlier about not wanting to wear out my singers. That's something crucial I learned from being on the receiving end of it. If you make singers rehearse full belt for three hours and then go straight into a concert, they will end up voiceless. That's also an important part of programme planning, constructing a concert so that it gives the singers time to recover from a taxing piece. If you're singing something like Arnold Bax's *Mater ora Filium*, it has to come at the end otherwise it will destroy the singers. That applies to what you cover in rehearsals too. If you have a lot of music to get through, sometimes it's enough just to run through it quickly, give pointers, and know which bits you need to cover thoroughly and which ones you can leave, trusting the singers to do it well in performance.

*I noticed that in the rehearsal of yours I sat in on, for the concert at Kings Place.*
Absolutely. In that rehearsal, I covered some things in detail – turning a corner, the pull-up of a phrase, the sense of the words going through a particular phrase – and other things I left. We recently performed Aaron Copland's *In the Beginning . . .* at the Aldeburgh Festival, and it's a big sing. We needed to rehearse the very end of the piece, but I didn't once ask them to sing it *fortissimo* in rehearsal, because I can trust them to do that in the concert, and I didn't want to

wear them out. In the end, the concert was electric, because they still had all the energy they needed. And sometimes, it's a question of knowing where in the texture to put your attention; rather than focusing on the sopranos who are singing high and loud, really work on developing the bass parts, so there is a vibrancy to the chord. In the Anglican world, that's a trap many conductors fall into, focusing only on the top line, the choristers, rather than on the altos, tenors and basses.

*You've spoken a few times about how personal the human voice is, and how emotional too. Singing is a vulnerable thing to do. Conducting strikes me as being rather like that too. Have you ever struggled with yourself as a conductor?*
Not really when it comes to conducting *a cappella* music. I have always known what I've wanted to do with a choir. In rehearsal, if something doesn't work, I will change it. If one of the singers makes a comment, I will think again, even if it's about something as simple as a breath or a tempo. I tend not to have to change my interpretation of the piece too much. But orchestrally, yes, I have struggled a bit. Particularly if it's a contemporary work with a lot of complex rhythms and time signatures, I have to work hard because I haven't had any real training.

*I wasn't so much talking about the practical struggle, as about the internal, psychological struggle.*
Well, I'm starting from quite a lucky place, because all the music I conduct is repertoire I love. I rarely have to do something I don't want to do. The time I've struggled most was the

first opera I did, Gluck's *Orfeo*. I really struggled with the accompanied recitative, which is a minefield. I was relieved to find out that most conductors find recitative very difficult to handle. You have to convey the meaning and flow of the text to orchestral players who don't have the words in front of them.

*That's still a practical struggle, though. What I'm talking about is more existential. I suppose my question comes from having interviewed a lot of conductors, all of whom at some point reveal that they have had periods of struggling with self-belief, because it's such a lonely and exposed job. They often talk about sitting in their dressing room, wondering if they have what it takes to stand up and lead their musicians.*

Well, I'm lucky that I haven't ever had that experience with The Sixteen, and I think that's because they've been mine since the start. I do worry if one of my musicians isn't performing or singing well, and I spend time sitting in my dressing room wondering about how to get the best out of them in performance. Or, during a performance, if I see someone isn't doing well, I have to think on my feet and figure out how to get the best out of them.

You talk about the loneliness, and it's true that there have been times, when I was doing a lot of freelance conducting abroad, that I have been lonely. I remember one time I was working in Bergen in Norway, the weather was awful, I didn't know a soul, I was in an apartment on my own, nothing on the television, and I was dying to get home. But the real problem there was that I didn't know anyone in the orchestra. Ultimately, I'm a sociable person. I have become better at being on my own over the years, and if I know that I'll be alone, I'll bring work with me. I go to Granada sometimes to conduct, and I've started to enjoy being in a beautiful place, wandering around, and having lunch on my own in the square. But being alone is certainly the time when I think about my life, about the future, and can start worrying.

*So you're saying that mostly you don't experience the loneliness of a conductor because your musicians are your friends, your family even?*
Absolutely. By nature, singers are sociable people. It was an interesting experience going to Boston for the first time, because it was a big organisation and I felt apart from the musicians in a way I hadn't experienced much before. I instantly wanted to get to know them and be a part of them, and to be able to talk to them.

Of course, knowing your musicians well as friends can be tricky too. There are people I've had to talk to about an aspect of their singing that isn't working, and those conversations are so hard. I will often put them off until things reach a point where I simply have to sort it out. It could be to do with their singing or their commitment, and these are really delicate things when people have livings to make and families to look after.

*I'm going to ask you one more difficult, probing question about conducting – I hope you don't mind. It's about ego. People often talk about the maestro's ego. One of your singers remarked to me that of course you have an ego, but you don't ever show it. Is that true?*
Oh, I don't know about ego. I don't feel that I have a massive

one. Lonnie might disagree; she certainly says I always have to be right. In fact, *she* is always right, so it's probably true. But having a big ego wasn't really valued in my upbringing. I have lived my life enjoying company rather than dominating it, I think. And I certainly don't regard The Sixteen as an environment where it's appropriate for me to have a big ego. I suppose the circumstances in Boston are slightly different, and because I feel more of a sense of responsibility, I have to gear myself up for a concert. But that's not really about ego, it's about going out there with a strong sense of purpose. Part of that is down to the audience, and their expectations of me; it's so academic there, they know their stuff, and I feel I'm being watched with a critical eye, which I have to try and block out. I feel I have to deliver. I feel that too with The Sixteen, but I have a different confidence with them.

*Given all we have discussed today, what do you think is the most important thing you have learned over the years about conducting?*

I suppose that over time, I have learned to find my voice by following the shape of the music. I have also learned to trust, and to do less. I have realised that I don't have to conduct every single bar. The young conductors I coach on Genesis Sixteen turn up wanting to bring in every single voice or cue in the polyphony. They will be meticulous about every single point, but forget that the phrase continues after that point. It's so important to concentrate on shaping the phrase. A phrase has to go somewhere beyond its pinnacle. I think that's also the defining thing about the sound of The Sixteen: that phrases go somewhere. My whole conducting style has been about that. Whatever I'm doing – be it Palestrina, Victoria, a Handel chorus – there will always be a special moment in the music that I make something of. The trick is to make something of it without it sounding overdone, always completely part of the music.

And the importance of breath. I go on and on about it to young conductors. Feel the breath in the music, make it a part of the music. It sounds like such a simple idea, but it's the most important thing, and it's much more difficult than one thinks. The piece I use as an example of this is Palestrina's famous *Missa Papae Marcelli*. I say to students, if you can master that piece, you can do anything. If you take a clinical approach to the piece and motor on through it, it will sound breathless. But if you allow too much breath and time at the end of every phrase, it sounds jolting, stopping and starting. Palestrina's music goes with the shape of the words. And with all good composers – it doesn't matter if it's Monteverdi, Tallis, Brahms, Bruckner or Britten – the principle remains: have faith in them, in the way that they wrote the music, and let it breathe.

# EIGHT
# The Future

Our final morning together is brief; Harry has meetings in town, and I have a baby to attend to. It is late June, and ferociously hot outside. Harry arrives promptly as always, with a warm greeting, and we sit as before, across from one another on sofa and armchair, with the garden doors wide open. I am struck by how full of ease our conversations have felt since the beginning, by how honest Harry has been, and how he has seemed to approach every question with a gesture of positivity and goodwill, even when I have probed and challenged in the direction of discomfort. As Julie Cooper so rightly said, Harry is a gentleman, and I feel sad that our time together is ending. Still, I have the sense that we have talked ourselves round to the beginning again.

We have chosen the final piece of music together, and it has taken some time, because there are so many possible works we haven't yet discussed which seem to define the group and Harry as a musician. But we finally settle on that captivating piece of Tudor polyphony I heard The Sixteen perform live in Kings Place: *Libera nos I* by John Sheppard.

It is a pleasure to listen to again, and it also gives me a chance to ask Harry more about how he put that programme together for Kings Place; how the sequence of works by Byrd, Palestrina and Lassus that came before it built an emotional arc which intensified the experience of the Sheppard. That is where our final conversation begins.

୨୬

*When I came to hear you in Kings Place, Harry, I was particularly moved by the trajectory of the first half of that concert. It began with slow and atmospheric pieces for Compline, and then the harmonic movement picked up, with busier works by Byrd and Lassus, and finally the emotional peak of the Sheppard. Can you tell me a bit about how you built the programme?*

I was asked to put it together specially for the Kings Place series, 'Time Unwrapped'. They asked me for a concert based on the Benedictine Office of the Day, the sequence of chant services which form the backbone of the day in a monastery. I found out what the responds and psalms of the day on which we were performing would be, and as much as possible tried to reflect those texts and plainsong in the pieces of polyphony we sang.

In the first half of the concert, the one you heard, I chose pieces that would build up nicely to the Sheppard, which is also rooted in plainsong. We began the concert with Victoria, one of his settings of the *Salve Regina*. The build-up you're talking about was really the result of a sequence of three pieces, all psalm settings from the office of the day, and a trajectory that becomes more and more vibrant and triumphant. It began with Byrd's *Oculi omnium*, which is very simple and in four parts, and rather reflective. The 'Alleluia' trio in the Byrd is rhythmic, but not ebullient like some of his music. Then came Palestrina's *Ecce nunc*, music that amazes me because of the beauty of its construction. He really is the master; you don't have to do anything to interpret his music because it's all done for you. If you just go with the shape of the words and trust Palestrina, it creates a soothing simplicity. And the Lassus Psalm 147 setting, *Lauda Jerusalem*, followed. I love Lassus, and I don't understand why people don't programme him more often. I have the feeling with this piece that it should be performed with sackbuts and cornets, which of course we don't have; so instead you have to sing it in a punchy way to convey that kind of sound. It is a festive psalm, but when I say punchy I don't mean really gung-ho. The tendency with that sort of music is to sing it loudly, but to really achieve the excitement of it, you have to build the phrases.

And then came the first of the two settings of *Libera nos* by Sheppard. Sheppard was at Magdalen, and this piece is so special for me. Again, we are back to the influence of David Wulstan. Sally Dunkley has often said that if David hadn't done all that research on Sheppard, we wouldn't know his music. It was very much David and The Clerkes of Oxenford who gave this music to twentieth-century audiences.

*Libera nos I* is an absolute gem. Almost all of Sheppard's music is based on a *cantus firmus*, a drawn-out section of plainsong that underpins the harmonic structure of the work. In this piece, unusually, the plainsong is in the bass. Normally it would be in the tenor, but it is his genius to lay it down, rather like a *basso continuo* line, and to let all the other parts luxuriate around it. The piece begins with a simple plainsong intonation, and then the basses start on the low *cantus firmus*. The first bar is static, the basses move up a note, and then begins some exquisite imitative tracery on the words 'Salva nos' – 'save us'. The music rocks from part to part in the words 'O beata Trinitas' – 'O beautiful Trinity'. Then the harmony seems to rest – and in performance I always bring the volume right down, a big *diminuendo*, so that the listener's ears really focus, and then it is as though the whole room sighs, and the music starts all over again. Really, this piece is my number one Desert Island Disc. It is so short, and so beautiful.

*You describe it so well. I was moved in your performance by the tempo, too – it seemed to unfold perfectly. How do you judge the tempo of that piece?*

The quavers have to emerge from the crotchet. They cannot be rushed, but they also shouldn't feel laboured or like you are wallowing in them. The crotchets also need a bit of movement to them.

*There are in fact two settings of* Libera nos, *and you did them both.*

The second one is often forgotten because the first is so gorgeous, but we put them together. That was what is thought to have happened at Magdalen, that the two settings were sung in sequence, with plainsong in between them, at the end of each day.

*You've been performing this piece for some time now. Presumably when you first did it, it was at the higher pitch. Did that make a difference to how it sounded?*

Yes, we have an old recording with Ruth Dean and Carolyn Sampson singing the top line, floating on B flats. When I saw the light about pitch, and started returning the music to the lower key, this is one of the pieces I worried about. I thought it might lose its ethereal, celestial quality, but in fact it didn't. The sonority of the middle of the texture is just heavenly, and I think it works because it is a real work of art.

*It feels Romantic to me, somehow – of course it's much earlier, but it has something of that sensibility, do you agree?*
Yes, you're right. That is partly to do with the harmony, but also Sheppard's mastery of word-painting. When I listen to it, it has the effect of making me breathe more deeply.

*I've enjoyed speaking with you about this piece. Let's end by taking stock of where you are now with The Sixteen, forty years on; but before we do, I want to talk about the choral scene more broadly in the UK. We touched on it briefly when discussing America, but I wanted to ask you in particular about what seems to be a real renaissance of interest in singing here. Some people call it the 'Gareth Malone effect', and it's now more visible than ever before. There is research into how beneficial singing is, mentally and physically. As someone who's been involved in choral singing your whole life, do you think there's been a renaissance?*
Yes, absolutely. And what is remarkable is that it has happened despite problems and cuts in education, from schools to cathedrals. In particular, there has been a surge in interest in amateur singing, particularly big choruses, and an emphasis on singing for fun. If you look back to years ago, every city had a big chorus that would be performing at Christmas, or singing a Passion at Easter. Even before Gareth

Malone came on the scene, there were more community choruses starting up, but his enthusiasm and public appeal on television have had a huge impact too. Singing in a chorus brings an enormous sense of camaraderie, just as being in a professional group like The Sixteen does.

In terms of sacred music, the story is different. We have seen many great cathedral choirs struggle over the last fifteen years, largely due to funding. There has been a particular drop in the so-called 'back row' of cathedral choirs: the lay clerks, the men's voices. Part of that is to do with the fact that those choirs previously expanded, throughout the 1970s and '80s. When I was in Canterbury, there were only three men on each side. The choir had two altos, two tenors and two basses in total. Canterbury now has a full complement of twelve. Then, during the 1990s, there were big financial problems, so many choirs had to cut back.

Over the last fifteen years or so, we have seen girls' choirs in cathedrals starting up, which is terrific. In some cases they have tried to mix girls' and boys' voices, which I don't think works. You can't mix the voices of boys and girls aged between eight and twelve, because the boy treble voice is such a unique sound. It is there for such a short-lived time, I think it is worth preserving it. But I am very much in support of having girls' choirs running alongside them. The quality of some of the girls' choirs out there is absolutely excellent. Most of the sopranos who have sung with The Sixteen haven't had the experience of being a chorister, and they have had to work hard at conservatoires and colleges, in order to develop their sight-reading skills. I am excited about the impact this new generation of girls' choirs will have on the standard of singing in the UK. We already have one regular soprano in the group, and a couple of excellent deps, who come from that background.

Meanwhile, the National Youth Choirs of Great Britain are on a real high at the moment; The Voices Foundation is also doing excellent things. A lot of cathedrals are offering bursaries for children from lower-income families so they have the opportunity to sing too. But all this is happening despite the diabolical state of music education in schools. My children went to local grammar schools; we were just lucky to have a lot of those schools near where we live. When my boys were at Judd Grammar School in Tonbridge, the school won an award for excellence in music. At the time, it had a choir and an orchestra. Now, it doesn't have a music department at all.

Over the last few years I have felt encouraged by all that is going on in these areas, particularly in the realm of community singing, but I have had a real concern for the future of the kind of singing which I'm involved in. That's why we started Genesis Sixteen, to train up the next generation if we couldn't guarantee the old model of cathedral and college singing could be sustained.

*Why is it, do you think, that we are seeing this interest in choral singing? Why now, and what's the appeal?*
Well, there's one very simple factor, which is that singing is cheap. You don't have to buy or loan an instrument. Everybody has a voice, and in fact now people are realising that everyone can sing, and better than they imagined. My wife Lonnie has recently taken over an amateur choir at a church

in Sevenoaks. She was looking for a congregational Mass to sing with them. In the end she found one by, as luck would have it, James MacMillan. It was perfect, because all the others she had been looking at went too high for the men – up to Ds. But listen to a football or rugby crowd; the singers are reaching up far higher than that. Put them in a church, and the men always sing an octave lower. So, what is the difference? It has to do with being in a different environment. Now that community singing is taking off in village halls, in local pubs, it's becoming more of a social thing, and bringing people together to do something that we all have the ability to do. And a lot of the success of this movement is down to the people who start it, their enthusiasm for getting choirs off the ground.

*Have you noticed the rise in interest in amateur choral singing having an impact on the audience you get for your concerts?*
Oh, very much so. There are always people who come up to us afterwards to tell us about their own choirs. I am also encouraged by how many young people seem to have caught the choral bug. We recently met some students at a concert in Exeter, one of whom had every single one of our Eton Choirbook CDs. That was so meaningful to me, because that was my aim right back at the start of The Sixteen: to bring this astonishing music to a wider public. And it seems to be working.

*So, forty years on, what is the appeal of the Eton Choirbook music, do you think? What does it have to offer to us – to that student – today?*

Let's start with the fact that this music is really good. Not only that, it was innovative in its day, and you can still hear that when you listen to it now. There is also a huge range of sound-worlds to explore within Renaissance polyphony. Back when we all started, there was a tendency to create a single sound-world so that everything sounded the same; but as we discussed in an earlier conversation, the polyphony of Sheppard is completely different to that of Victoria. So there is a wealth of music to discover.

And I think that for today's listeners, this music has a spirituality that is attractive. Our world is not ostensibly spiritual anymore, but everybody has a spirit, and a spiritual nature, and I think that the concert-going public finds a more modern connection to the sacred spirituality of this music. When it's well performed – and done with immediacy, which I hope The Sixteen always achieves – it connects with people's emotions, it challenges them and enriches their lives. I am constantly hearing our audience confirm that, and I find that very powerful.

I'm aware that when I talk about spirituality and challenge in the same breath, that might sound like a contradiction. I notice that a lot of contemporary choral music that considers itself spiritual has gone back to a simpler, homophonic style, which is effective, but nothing like the innovative, wacky extremes of Byrd or Josquin.

*You think part of the appeal of polyphony is its complexity?*
Yes. When people hear Brumel's 'Earthquake' Mass or Tallis's *Spem in alium* they are blown away. Both are incredibly complex in their own way. The audience who heard us perform

William Cornysh's *Salve Regina* in a Choral Pilgrimage gasped at its complexity. That piece transports you somewhere completely different; and then you get to the end, and it's suddenly angular, vertical, rhythmic singing, with the voices answering one another. It's incredibly complex, and people find it amazing. I think Cornysh would be incredibly proud to know his music still had that impact today.

*So, let's take stock of The Sixteen. How are you feeling about your fortieth-anniversary celebrations next year?*
It feels quite wonderful. I never dreamt that The Sixteen would get where it is today. The Choral Pilgrimage is central to our concert output each year, and in 2019 we will be looking back to where we started, with a large-scale piece by Robert Fayrfax, and the Wylkynson *Salve Regina*. We are also looking forward with Jimmy's new piece, and others by Eric Whitacre and Gabriel Jackson. In the same year, we're performing Claudio Monteverdi's 1610 Vespers, a piece that is very important to me. We haven't even touched on Monteverdi, but he is crucial to me and my work as a musician. We'll be performing his *Selva morale e spirituale* at Wigmore Hall. We're also staging Handel's *Belshazzar* at the Grange Festival, and we are part of a new symphony which Jimmy is writing for the Edinburgh International Festival. The symphony is called *Le Grand Inconnu*, and is about the Holy Spirit. I haven't seen it yet – it's very exciting. The association we have with Jimmy is going from strength to strength. So, it will be a very exciting and busy year for us.

*How do you feel about the fact that it has continued for forty years, despite you never dreaming of it?*
It's lovely. I adore seeing how it has grown and taken off, and really, it's about the people who have been part of it. After forty years, the choir is totally bedded down and is singing at its best. I love the variety of projects we are doing, and while I always say that the musical repertoire we do reflects my own taste, I feel there is so much music out there still to do. I have devised the next two or three years of Choral Pilgrimage programmes already.

*What are your ambitions for the group?*
I would say that my ambitions are all being realised. I want us to carry them on, to keep our concert life going and the record company afloat. There are a lot of hurdles out there, not least the state of the recording industry, but I am determined. And I would like to keep on doing special projects on top of our regular season, like the Sistine Chapel appearance, or the Streetwise Opera *Passion* project we did in 2016, a life-changing experience for everyone involved.

*We haven't even touched on that project; it seems there is indeed always more to talk about than there is time. A final question, Harry, and one I feel a little awkward asking . . . Do you think The Sixteen could survive without you?*
I hope it would. Of course I want to keep on doing it until I can't anymore, but if I went under a bus tomorrow, the board would make sure to keep it going, and they would choose someone to continue my work. I really wouldn't want it to end; I want the legacy to carry on. Whoever did

take over, I would hope they would find their own way with it, but still maintain the principles of the group. The Sixteen today is a wonderful group of people, very thoughtful and supportive of one another. They are basically a family, and I would hope that, above all, would continue.

# Listening

The following eight works prompted our discussions, and are listed here with the details of the corresponding CD recording should you wish to listen yourself; all but one can be found on Harry's CORO label. In some cases, Harry's recording with The Sixteen appears on more than one disc; where possible I have listed the option that contains more music by the same composer.

CHAPTER ONE
Thomas Tallis: *O nata lux*
*An Immortal Legacy*, CORO16111

CHAPTER TWO
William Mundy: *Vox Patris caelestis*
*The Voice of the Turtle Dove*, CORO16119

CHAPTER THREE
Francis Poulenc: *Figure humaine*
*Francis Poulenc: Sacred Works*, ERATO 5624312

CHAPTER FOUR
Tomás Luis de Victoria: *Vadam et circuibo*
*The Call of the Beloved: Tomas Luis de Victoria*, CORO16007

# Acknowledgements

I am indebted to Belinda Matthews for inviting me to take part in this project in the first place, and for steering it with such a light and kindly hand.

I am deeply grateful to Belinda and Harry for their patience with me as I navigated early motherhood and book deadlines. I could not have managed it without the help of my daughter's father, Sam Lee, and both our families. Chris Mohr did valiant childcare while Harry and I talked, as did Anna Mohr-Pietsch, Hans Pietsch and Stephanie Lee while I typed. Thanks also to Rosie Bradford, Clemency Burton-Hill, Hannah Mulder, Andrew Dickson, Lara Feigel, Juliet Fraser, Anna Kenyon, Fiona Maddocks, Miriam Manook, Peter Meanwell, Kate Molleson, Tom Service and Joanna Potts for their support and advice.

I experienced enormous warmth and generosity from Harry's family too, particularly his wife Veronica, who welcomed me into their home during a harsh winter; and indeed from his other family, the singers of The Sixteen. Eamonn Dougan, Sally Dunkley and Julie Cooper were kind enough to stay behind after a long rehearsal, and put up with a screaming baby as we talked. Marie-Sophie Willis, the group's Chief Executive, was extremely helpful with my requests for information and concert tickets, as were Jessica Tomkins, their Marketing Manager, and Cath Edwards, who runs CORO.

But above all, my thanks go to Harry himself for giving of his time and his thoughts so generously. If you ever find yourself at one of his concerts, make sure to go up to him afterwards. He is a pleasure to talk to.

# Index